Public Employee Unionism
in Belgium

COMPARATIVE STUDIES IN PUBLIC EMPLOYMENT LABOR RELATIONS

Public Employee Unionism
in Belgium

ROGER ⌊BLANPAIN
UNIVERSITY OF LEUVEN LAW SCHOOL

ANN ARBOR
INSTITUTE OF LABOR AND INDUSTRIAL RELATIONS
THE UNIVERSITY OF MICHIGAN—WAYNE STATE UNIVERSITY
1971

This monograph is one of a series prepared under the direction of Professors Russell A. Smith and Charles M. Rehmus of The University of Michigan, and is a part of their comparative international study of labor relations in public employment. Financial support of this research project has been derived from a number of sources. Basic grants came from the comparative law research funds of The University of Michigan Law School; the Institute of Labor and Industrial Relations, The University of Michigan—Wayne State University; the comparative economics research funds of The University of Michigan Economics Department; and the research programs of the New York State Public Employment Relations Board and the United States Department of Labor.

Preface

TRADE unionism in the Belgian public sector has up to
now been somewhat neglected both in the teaching field
and in research. Different reasons may be advanced here; a general one is the legalistic attitude to research prevailing in many
European countries, emphasizing only legal rules and not taking
into account the realities of the situation. As in so many aspects
of labor relations, law and reality may be two different affairs,
especially in the public sector. A further reason, beyond doubt,
is the semisecrecy and the almost inextricable web of red tape
and administrative decrees with which labor relations problems
in the public sector are shrouded. So many political and ideological "deals" have been made, which combined with inherited
practice, give the impression that logic has almost been eluded.
Another cause must be found in the still-prevalent view held
by most academicians of a divorce between the public and
private sector. The study of labor law or labor relations is con-
fined to the private sector, and while labor relations in the public
sector should be dealt with in administrative law, the subject
is almost completely neglected.

It is clear that many of these factors will be reflected in the
following pages. Perhaps more problems will be raised than
solved. Nevertheless, we have tried to go into the realities of
labor relations in the public sector, eager to find out what is going
on, less concerned with the legal niceties and constructions of
which European lawyers are so fond. The purpose of this paper
is to identify and underline basic rules and principles of public
sector labor relations in Belgium. Both the legal rules and the
working principles will be underlined with an emphasis which
oversimplifies and overstates. This is deliberate, for comprehen-
siveness or pedantic accuracy would obscure the basic structure.

Because labor relations in general are part of and shaped
by the social and cultural environment from which they emanate,
Chapter I covers aspects of Belgian history, its cultural and
political system, and the prevailing values in Belgian society.
We will also consider the private sector labor relations system
of the country, since solutions for comparable or identical problems in this sector have an increasing influence in the pattern

set for the public sector. Chapter II deals with some characteristics and data of the civil service, the labor force in the public sector, collective bargaining developments, and other features. Chapter III provides a description of the trade unions in the public sector: trade union freedom, structure, degree of organization, relationship between public sector and private sector unions, and the recognition of trade unions. A brief description of the Belgian political and administrative system is also given. In Chapter IV the institutionalized relations between trade union and public employer will be discussed. The traditional pattern (advisory function) and the new pattern (bargaining function) will also be examined. Chapter V deals with collective bargaining in the public sector, the impact of the cabinet system, and the centralization of decision making in collective bargaining. We will cover the bargaining itself as it is conducted by the way of national "social programmation" agreements, covering the public sector as a whole and sectorial agreements. Finally, the freedom to strike and the settlement of industrial disputes will be examined in Chapter VI.

Many organizations and individuals have contributed to the research for this study for which I am deeply grateful. To name them individually would be an impossible task, but I must acknowledge however a special debt to Mr. O. Vanachter, research assistant at the Institute for Labor Relations, who helped me enormously in the gathering of documentation.

R. BLANPAIN

March 1, 1970

Contents

Public Employee Unionism
in Belgium

· I ·

Labor Relations in the
Private Sector

IT is commonplace that no labor relations system can be grasped completely without taking in account the cultural and historical environment in which the system has its roots.[1] This is certainly the case for a country like Belgium, in which the Communist Manifesto was published in 1848, where the Socialist movement has had a large following, where the Catholic religion had a deep impact, and where Liberalism was a strong force in the nineteenth century.

Labor relations, generally in Europe but especially in Belgium, are still marked by ideological differences. The different trade unions pursue conflicting principles on such issues as the role of the state in public life, the role of private enterprise, nationalization of industries, and the programs and goals of the educational system, and they seek to influence the views of Belgian society as a whole on such issues. Ideological conflicts are so deeply rooted that trade unions themselves are integrated parts of the political, social, and cultural movements effecting the society generally. Political parties and cultural organizations, which share and defend the same beliefs, also belong to these larger movements. Although lately ideological differences are emphasized less sharply than before and a pragmatic approach prevails in some matters, opposed ideologies still remain influential factors in the development of the dynamics of Belgian society and labor relations. They explain many realities which otherwise would be completely misunderstood or not grasped at all. An example is the prevalent pluralism of trade unions, which contrasts with the unity of employer associations in Belgium.

1. See further, A. Kamin, ed., *Western European Labor and the American Corporation.* Washington, Bureau of National Affairs, 1969, pp. 209-52; also Seyfarth, Shaw, Fairweather & Geraldson, *Labor Relations and the Law in Belgium and the United States,* Michigan International Labor Studies. Ann Arbor, Bureau of Business Research, Graduate School of Business Administration, The University of Michigan, 1968.

3

LABOR RELATIONS IN THE PRIVATE SECTOR

Labor relations in Belgium are largely dominated by the two major trade unions, the Socialists and the Christians, which are almost omnipresent. On the national, interprofessional, or interindustrial level, they participate in the shaping of national economic and social policies through formal consultation, generally at the request of the public authorities. On the industrial level they are represented in the joint committees in which industry-wide collective agreements are made with binding effect for the industry as a whole. On the level of the enterprise they are represented through union delegations, working councils, and safety and health committees, all of which are more fully described below.

The close links of major trade unions with the major political parties and the parliamentary membership and even government membership of a large number of actual or former trade union leaders are also characteristic of Belgian labor relations. It is a truism that if both the Socialist and the Christian trade unions support an issue, they can have it pushed through parliament rather easily. This explains the constant political influences upon Belgian labor relations. The political power of trade unions explains the extensive protective labor legislation, the absence of legislation regulating trade unions, and the existence of the almost absolute freedom to strike.

Another significant feature of Belgian labor relations is organized participation in public life and even collaboration between trade unions and employer associations, especially the Federation of Belgian Industries, on national and industry-wide levels. This working relationship is the result of a long evolution in which the events of World War II played an important and special role. In the last months of the war, union leaders and the representatives of the employers associations made a secret agreement in which they established the main principles upon which a modern labor relations system would be founded. The pact, which was very explicit, was a blueprint describing the main points of social reform to be developed in the postwar period. It concerned wages, hours of work, social security (pensions, sickness and invalidism, unemployment, family allowances, annual vacation), the establishment of union delegations, joint committees, and a national joint council, and the settlement of industrial disputes. This working relationship led in 1960 to agreements, called "programmation," by which social progress, taking into account economic possibilities, was jointly planned by employers and trade unions at the national interindustrial level as well as at the industrial level.

Collective labor relations in Belgium rely almost entirely on practices and de facto agreements between the social partners, i.e., labor and management. There is no significant legislation on collective bargaining, strikes, settlement of industrial disputes, and the like. An important feature of the Belgian system is that trade unions have no legal personality, which means among other things that they cannot be sued and in fact are not sued in court for breach of collective agreements. The existing legislation, including the most recent Act of 1968, has, with qualifications, reflected rather than influenced practices.

Although labor relations in Belgium may appear chaotic, in general, the pragmatic approach which prevails seems to have quite satisfactory results, as indicated by the low number of lost working days through strikes. Lawyers do not play any substantial role in the negotiation and administration of collective agreements or in the settlement of industrial conflicts. Unions are rather jealous of their system and openly and frankly resist any imported changes. Nevertheless, the system is by and large quite elastic and leaves to management a great deal of freedom in exercising its managerial functions.

TRADE UNIONS

Almost 65 percent of Belgian workers belong to trade unions, thus putting Belgium first in the degree of unionization in the European Economic Community. Italy has 43 percent, Germany and Luxembourg 37 percent, and the Netherlands 34 percent. In France 26.5 percent of the eligible workers are union members[2].

The most important trade unions are the Confederation of

2. D. Sauer, *Europa en de vakbeweging,* Leuven, 1966, p. 15 (proef-schrift).

Christian Trade Unions (ACV-CSC)[3] and the Socialist Trade Union Movement (ABVV-FGTB).[4] Less important is the Liberal Trade Union Movement (ACLV-CGLSB).[5] Of the total active employee population of 2,863,500 in 1965 (1,974,600 male workers and 888,900 female workers), about 1.7 million were organized as follows according to union estimates: Christian trade unions, about 840,000; Socialist trade unions, about 775,000; Liberal trade unions, 80,000 to 100,000.[6]

In the major sectors of industry, such as metals, chemicals, cement, petroleum, and mines, almost 90 percent of the blue-collar workers are organized. White-collar workers tend to organize less (approximately 40 percent), while staff or supervisory personnel are rarely organized, although they have under the 1921 Act a legal right to do so and under the 1968 Act to bargain collectively.

Belgian trade unions are not organized on a craft or occupational basis. Industrial unions prevail. Both the Socialist and Christian unions have divisions for white-collar workers only, whatever may be the sector of industry to which they belong.

The FGTB is based on the principles of democratic socialism, which correspond with those of the Belgian Socialist Party. Its declared goal is a system of social and economic democracy under which the production apparatus will be at the service of the whole community. Fourteen national unions are affiliated with the FGTB. Each union is an independent organization with its own structure, governing bodies, and statutory rules. To become affiliated, the union must give assurance that it will accept the basic principles of the Socialist FGTB, and that it will carry out all the decisions made by the governing bodies of the FGTB. The Socialist trade union movement is completely free in its organizational activities and cannot be forced to give

3. Algemeen Christelijk Vakverbond—Confédération des Syndicats Chrétiens.
4. Algemeen Belgisch Vakverbond—Fédération Générale du Travail de Belgique.
5. Algemeen Centrale der Liberale Vakbonden—Centrale Générale des Syndicats Liberaux de Belgique.
6. R. Blanpain, *Handboek van het Belgisch Arbeidschrecht*. Gent, 1968, p. 185.

an account of conduct that accords with the basic FGTB principles and governing rules. On the contrary, the FGTB is the only Socialist body authorized to make decisions on the general or national level in defense of the general interests of the workers. The socialist trade union movement is decentralized at regional and local levels. The FGTB participates in the "Socialist Common Action," which was created in 1950. The Socialist Common Action coordinates the various branches of the socialist movement—Coop-Health Institutions, FGTB and Socialist Party—and is the discussion center on the principal problems of concern to the whole socialist movement.

The Christian workers in Belgium are grouped in a national organization called the Christian Labor Movement.[7] The aim of this organization is to defend the interests of the workers in accordance with Christian social doctrine and the principles of democracy. It is composed of specialized national organizations for economic, cultural and educational action such as the Confederation of Christian Trade Unions (CSC), mutual insurance companies, cooperative societies, Workers' Youth, Women's Guild, and the Workers' Associations.

The CSC is the nationwide organization entrusted with the direction of the activities of all Christian trade unions in Belgium. The CSC in the main has the same structure as the FGTB. It is composed of 17 national unions based on industry, which are also decentralized on a regional and a local level.

The Christian, Socialist, and Liberal Unions are recognized by the government as being the "most representative unions" of the totality of the workers. Other minority trade unions are almost completely excluded from any possible trade activity. Only the three unions mentioned are represented in the various economic, social, and financial institutions and bodies. They alone have the right to present candidates for elections to working councils, health and safety committees at the plant level or for nomination in the joint committees at the industry level. In practice, only the CSC and the FGTB are the significant "partners" with which the employers must deal on all levels.

7. Algemeen Christelijk Verkersverbond—Mouvement Ouvrier Chrétien.

Trade Union Freedom

Freedom to join or not to join a union is guaranteed by the Act of May 1921 (Appendix 1). According to Article 1 of this Act, "no person shall be compelled to join or refrain from joining any association." However, a punishable infraction of the law depends upon proof of "criminal" intent to infringe upon the freedom of association. This act requires a *dolus specialis* (specific intent), which is extremely difficult to prove. Only about 10 prosecutions have been undertaken since 1921.

In practice, yellow-dog contracts as well as union-security clauses such as closed shop, union shop, agency shop, and maintenance of membership, are almost unknown in Belgian labor relations. With few exceptions, checkoff is not practiced because unions do not want employers to know how many members they have. Unions prefer to collect dues from the members themselves at the place of work in Walloon country or at their homes in Flanders, in order to maximize personal contact and learn firsthand of complaints of members.

Devices exist, nevertheless, designed to persuade employees to join the representative unions. One device, common during the past ten years, is the stipulation in collective agreements for special benefits, or bonuses, for union members only. These take varied forms including supplemental retirement and unemployment compensation benefits. The *quid pro quo* to the employer is usually a no-strike (peace obligation) clause.[8] Unions have also successfully argued that a situation under which non-dues-paying, nonunion members also benefit, pursuant to the normative effect of general provisions of collective arguments, from trade union accomplishments financed by the dues and contributions of members is no longer acceptable, and thus it is just and equitable that a special benefit in the form of dues reimbursement bonus, paid by the employer, should be reserved

8. The reservation of benefits is not inconsistent with the principle by which collective agrements result in extension of the general benefits of such agreements to nonunion members. This results from the "normative" concept applied to collective bargaining; but the contracting parties are free to limit the scope of the agreement and do this, in the case of reserved benefits, in favor of union members.

solely to the union or to the union members. Although this union solidarity demand has been vigorously resisted by many employers, almost one million workers are covered by such clauses. The amount of the benefit or partial dues reimbursement varies from BF250 ($5.00) a year to BF1,500 ($30.00). Union dues in Belgium are quite low.

The building trade unions reject the idea of reserved benefits for union members. However, the administrative formalities and red tape in the Belgian construction industry are so complicated that unionization is virtually a necessity for workers, as is the formation of associations for employers. The availability of special financial allowances paid through a special social fund by collective agreement in case of layoff for bad weather alone is sufficient to convince building tradesmen of the merits of unionization.

Trade Union Structure

The CSC and the FGTB have essentially the same structure. Both are federations of national trade unions organized on behalf of industry, trade, or service. Fourteen national unions are affiliated with the FGTB, 17 with the CSC. I regard as superfluous an analysis of the Liberal Union Movement, which has little practical influence.

The CSC (Christian) unions are divided among the following groups: food industry; utilities; chemical industry; leather industry; diamond, paper, and printing industries; building and timber industries; metal industry; coal mining; public office; railroad, telephone, and telegraph industries; stone, cement, and glass industries; textile and garment industries; teamsters; clerical workers; teachers in primary schools; teachers in technical schools; teachers in public high schools; and teachers in free high schools.

Unions within the FGTB are the General Workers' Union; the white-collar workers' unions and the show business union as well as separate unions for the following industries or sectors: paper and printing; diamond; garment; textile; metal; coal mining; tramways; transport; food and public services.

Each national trade union is autonomous in defending the

interests of its members and discharging essential trade union functions. The national trade unions have provincial, regional, and local sections. The FGTB and the CSC have 24 and 33 regional federations, respectively. The regional federations which are subordinate bodies of the national federation coordinate the activities of the different trade unions operating within the region. For the most part, they are charged with administrative and financial duties such as the recruiting of new members, collection of dues, legal assistance to members, and propaganda.

Jurisdictional or demarcation disputes between national trade unions belonging to the same national federation are resolved through a binding decision taken within the central committee of the federation. There are no jurisdictional disputes between the parallel organizations of CSC and FGTB. Both deal with the employer or employers' associations in a common front. This means that the unions will bargain with the employer on the basis of a "common" program. First the several unions will draft their separate programs, then meet together and formulate a "common" program, which they will present jointly to the employer(s). Both are equally recognized by the employer side of the bargaining table. Of course, each movement seeks to attract as many members as possible. The relative strength of each union is reflected in the elections of working councils and health committees discussed later in this paper.

Most Representative Unions

Belgian labor relations cannot be understood without a full grasp of the practical meaning and consequences of what is called the "most representative trade union."[9] As noted earlier, only three unions, the Christian, the Socialist, and the Liberal, are recognized to be most representative by the government on a national basis as well as by the employers' associations.

The most representative trade unions enjoy a legal and a practical monopoly in representing the interests of the workers at the national level, the industry level, and the level of the enterprise or undertaking. They are the only ones to be represented

9. See Seyfarth, Shaw, Fairweather & Geraldson on most representative trade unions.

in the officially organized joint organs, composed of employers and employee representatives, in which a great deal of collective bargaining is done. At the national interprofessional level or interindustrial level this is the National Labor Council, at industry-wide level the joint committee, and at the enterprise level the working council and the health and safety committee.

The most representative unions, practically speaking only the Christian and Socialist unions, must be dealt with as the authorized and duly empowered bargaining spokesmen of employees. They cannot be excluded at the level of the enterprise by means of devices known to American or Canadian law, such as an election among eligible employee voters by which a majority union would be sole and exclusive bargaining representative of the employees or in which union representation would be altogether rejected.

Union Democracy and Administration

There is nothing in Belgian labor law comparable to the American Landrum-Griffin Act. Belgian unions are completely free and sovereign in all matters. Trade union leaders are not directly elected but are appointed by co-option, that is, by their predecessors in office, when vacancies occur, by those already in power.

The CSC describes the existing system as follows:[10]

> In the heroic times of the trade union movement, trade union leaders were nominated directly by the members, who selected for positions of leadership the most eloquent among their comrades and those who displayed the greatest dynamism and the liveliest zeal for trade union interests. These were the times of direct democracy in the management of trade union affairs. But with the further development of membership, the growing complexity of trade unions, and the centralization of trade union action caused by changes in industrial life, it proved no longer possible for the leaders to be elected directly by the members. First of all, not all members attend meetings; furthermore, ordinary members

10. Het Algemeen Christelyk Vakverbond, Brussel, p. 25.

are not always capable of forming a sound judgment of the aptitudes required of possible leaders. Direct elections, therefore, was replaced by appointment, by delegation and by cooptation.

Full-time officers are nominated by the Committee of the organization in whose service they are employed and their appointment has to be confirmed either by the Central Committee (Trades Centers and Regional Federations) or the Council (CSC). They are paid by their organization and relieved of all other professional activities.

At the top of the trade union hierarchy, we find those full-time officers who are entrusted with the direction of the Trades Centers, the Regional Federations and the CSC. They are recruited from among full-time officers of the second echelon and their nomination must also meet with the approval either of the Central Committee, or the Council of the organization concerned.

For the most part, rank-and-file members are not involved in the elaboration of union programs or in the establishment of the dues schedules. They have no right to examine financial documents and reports, which are kept secret. Trade unions claim that, notwithstanding the aforementioned procedures, there is a high degree of informal democracy; that trade union leaders come to the forefront through their zeal for the trade union cause and are readily accepted by the members; that union funds and especially the strike fund must be kept secret; and that employers above all should not know the financial strength and possibilities of the unions in cases of economic showdowns.

Whatever the merits of this reasoning, trade union members have a rather strong weapon in that in Belgium, the majority-union system is unknown and dissatisfied members may shift to the Socialist, Liberal, or Christian union. Ideology is incidental. Many employees join and remain with a particular union, less for adherence to the fundamental principles of *Rerum Novarum, Quadragesimo Anno,* or the Marxist-Socialist doctrine than for the practical bread-and-butter services rendered by the union.

The Legal Status of Trade Unions

Belgian trade unions have no formal legal status or corporate capacity, and collective agreements usually are not legally binding between the collective contracting parties and as such are not judicially enforceable. Lacking corporate capacity, unions cannot be sued if they do not fulfill their peace obligations, even when the obligation is explicitly stated in the collective agreement. Nor may the union in its own name sue the employer or the employer association for failure to perform obligations under the collective agreement. This situation may seem deplorable—and it is, according to many observers—but it will not change within the near future. It is also for this reason that employers—looking for some guarantees regarding the execution and administration of collective agreements have geared the payment of "benefits" reserved to union members, discussed earlier, directly to the faithful performance of the collective agreement and the maintenance of social peace during the life of the agreement.

The best example to be given in order to illustrate this point concerns the metalworking industry. In this sector the agreements contain the explicit clause that neither on the level of the enterprise nor on local, regional, or national level will claims of a general or collective nature be made during the life of the agreement. This clause, however, does not exclude individual wage adaptations and the examination of exceptional cases.

Neither a strike nor a lock-out can be called for before the elaborate procedure of conciliation, worked out by agreement between social partners, has been exhausted. However, if a strike breaks out without respecting the conciliation procedure, trade unions have the responsibility of getting workers back to work within a period of three days. If the unions fail to do so they may not support the concerned employees in any way whatsoever.

In return for safeguarding social peace trade unions receive from the employers, through the employers' association which collects the money, a financial "subvention" of 0.6 percent of gross wages. If the trade unions support wildcat striking employees, the subvention will be diminished by an amount equal to $2.50 per day per striking employee; this amount will be an amount equal to $5.00 if the strike continues for more than 20 days.

Exception is made when a strike breaks out due to the fact that an employer does not live up to the collective agreements. A board, composed of impartial civil servants chosen by the partners will decide in case of disagreement whether a collective agreement was or was not violated by the employer.

The agreements in the metalworking industry are by no means an exception in Belgian labor relations. Comparable relationships exist in the steel, petroleum, textile, and building industries as well as in others. This corresponds also to another main characteristic of Belgian industrial relations: labor relations are in the first place the responsibility of the social partners. The role of the government remains of secondary importance.

INSTITUTIONALIZED RELATIONS BETWEEN EMPLOYERS AND TRADE UNIONS

Interaction between organized labor and employers has resulted in degrees of institutionalization of labor relations at different levels. This working relationship between labor and employers is the result of a long historical development which started at the end of the last century.

At the level of the enterprise or establishment, three different bodies, representing both the employers and the trade unions, may operate. These are the union delegations, the working council, and the safety and health committee.

Joint committees function at the industry level. The National Labor Council, created in 1952, functions at the national interprofessional or interindustrial level. These unique institutions are the consequence of acceptance by employers that trade unions are their natural partners both inside and outside the business undertaking. It must be stressed that not all of these institutions are commanded by law. For example, the union delegation is entirely the product of collective bargaining. Even in legally obligatory bodies, working rules and practical matters are generally regulated by collective partners in accordance with the immediate and long-range needs of the enterprise or the industry, rather than by legal mandates.

Representation at Enterprise Level

The "triad" of the union delegation, the working council, and the safety and health committee that functions at the enterprise level is the result of compromise between the competitive attitudes of the major unions. The Christian unions favor the idea of collaboration between worker and management through the working council, and the Socialist trade unions emphasize the competition between labor and capital through the union delegation. A typical Belgian solution solved the problem. Not two but three organs were created where many agreed that one could do the job. It follows that there is a great deal of overlapping in practice regarding both the jurisdiction and the composition of the different bodies. In many cases, the same employees are simultaneously members of the union delegation, the working council, and the health and safety committee.

THE UNION DELEGATION

The union delegation is the product of collective bargaining. The delegation was first sketched in the postwar pact of social solidarity described above. The pact, which was very explicit, was a blueprint describing the main points of social reform to be developed in the postwar period. To assure union recognition at the plant level, a union delegation was to be created in every enterprise with more than 20 employees.

In June 1947 a national interindustry collective agreement was concluded between the social partners in which the main principles concerning the inauguration and the work of the union delegations were formulated. Each joint committee was asked to adapt these principles to the specific situations of the industry sector. More than 40 agreements were concluded in different industries and many more at the level of the enterprise or establishment.

The employer is not legally obliged to recognize a union delegation in his enterprise, but unions will ask him to do so if they have sufficient strength in the establishment to press such a claim. Union delegates are employees. They are sometimes elected by their fellow workers, but more frequently they are appointed by regional trade union officers. The number of the delegates varies with the size of the enterprise. In most cases there are separate delegations for manual workers and for white-collar workers. That union delegates are elected on different lists or are designated by different unions does not mean that the union delegation does not act as a whole. Generally, a chief delegate is chosen from the strongest union in the enterprise and acts as a spokesman for the group. When unions have about equal strength, two chief delegates are usually named.

The union delegate is the Belgian equivalent of an American shop steward, but he has little of the authority and power of a British shop steward. He presents and discusses grievances and otherwise supervises the application of collective agreements and labor law standards in the enterprise. It is sometimes claimed that in his actions within the enterprise, the union delegate is actually less autonomous than before, by becoming to a greater degree the mere deputy of the union in the enterprise, and that consequently he relies more heavily than in the past on the regular union business agent. However, in my view, the trade union succeeds or fails with the union delegation. This body is the favorite of all trade unions. They have such strong feelings about their delegates that they strongly resist the termination or disruption of their employment. In practice union delegates enjoy almost complete stability of employment.

WORKING COUNCIL

The employer is legally obliged under the Act of September 1948 to establish a working council when his enterprise regularly employs an average of 150 persons, including supervisory or leading personnel. The council is composed of a number of elected employee representatives and an equal number of employer representatives chosen by the employer from among his supervisory personnel.

Elections must be held every four years under legally detailed procedures. At the election, the Minister of Labor allots each of the three representative trade unions a number. Only the three representative unions have a right to present candidates. These candidates participate in the election at the level of the enterprise with the allotted number of their respective trade union. The available seats of delegates and substitute delegates are divided between blue-collar workers and white-collar workers according to their respective numerical strength in the establishment. All workers, whether members of a union or not, participate in the elections with the exception of leading or supervisory personnel, who have neither the right to vote nor the right to be candidates.

The purpose of the working council is to promote "collaboration" between the employees and the employer. The Act of 1948 enumerates functions of the working council. The council has the right to receive from the employer regular information on corporate financial and economic data, including productivity ratings of the various categories of workers. Every three months an oral progress report must be given, and at the end of the year the employer must supply a written progress report, together with such accounting information as the balance sheet and profit and losses. However, since the law is vague, and even requires some information which is impossible to compile, and since the employer is naturally reticent in giving financial and economic information, I say without hesitation that this part of the law has been unsuccessful. It is equally true that, notwithstanding a great effort by trade unions, many worker delegates are not able to understand fully the information that is delivered to them. It is also true that some are not really interested in the overall financial picture of the undertaking, as long as their own jobs and earnings are not affected.

In principle, the Act upholds the right of the workers' delegates to ask an auditor to check the financial and economic information given by the employer. In practice, however, this provision has little effect, for the task of the auditor is limited to a declaration as to whether the information given by the employer is complete and correct. Without the consent of the employer, the auditor cannot give any further information to the employee members of the working council. But, above all, the employer is usually the auditor's client and will be quite guarded in supplying information. It is not surprising that, in order to get complete financial and economic information, the trade unions today urge the promulgation of uniform legal rules of accounting and a thorough reform of the statute regarding company auditors.

The working council also has an advisory function concerning working conditions, productivity, and the examination of general criteria related to hiring and, more importantly, firing of employees.

The role of the working council is limited to giving suggestions. The right of ultimate decision remains completely with management. Unions accept the advisory role, but criticize the fact that many measures that result in changed working conditions at the job, such as automation and other work revisions to increase productivity, are taken without previous consultation with the enterprise council.

Finally, the working council has a function of codetermination in making work rules which generally bind the employer and employees, fixing dates of annual vacations for employees, and the direction of the welfare works of the enterprise in the cultural and social activities, recreation, sports, and the like.

Workers' delegates enjoy a great stability of employment and can only be dismissed for just cause under the law of 1948 as amended in January 1967, e.g., fighting, stealing, or other offenses familiar to those who read American grievance arbitration cases—or for technical or economical reasons, which must meet criteria recognized by the joint committee. The remedy for illegal discharge of a delegate or substitute is not reinstatement with possible back pay but the payment of an indemnification according to established scale: two years of wages when the delegate has less than ten years of service in the enterprise, three years when the delegate has from ten to twenty years' service, and four years when he has more than twenty years' service. The working councils have been most effective in protecting their delegates and substitutes and also in handling disputes concerning layoff and firing of rank-and-file personnel.

It is generally agreed that the working council has not had the success visualized by its creators. To what degree has the working council realized the idea of codetermination proposed by social reformers as an ultimate goal? My answer is not at all. First, economic and financial information and even suggestions are in many cases almost farcical, and the workers are not really interested in them. Information and suggestions are considered as debating points when jobs and livelihoods may be in danger. Comparatively speaking, it is my impression that in many ways American workers get more effective codetermination through collective bargaining than their Belgian counterparts get through formal and legal codetermination procedures.

THE SAFETY AND HEALTH COMMITTEE

Pursuant to a statute of June 10, 1952, a health and safety committee must be established by the employer when the enterprise employs more than 50 persons. The safety committee has a format much like the working council: elected employee members who enjoy equivalent job-stability guarantees and supervisory personnel nominated by the employer. The physician head of the medical service, a nurse, or even a social worker may assist at the meetings, as an expert without the right to vote. The safety committee must examine accident reports, attend to the application of the safety and health legislation, and develop means of propaganda and other proper measures to improve the safety and health of the workers in the establishment. The safety committee has no right of decision since the responsibility for safety and health rests with the employer. But the employer must eventually explain to the safety council and the state inspectors why a proposal agreed upon in the safety committee was not applied. Observers agree that the activities of the safety committees have been successful.

This short description of the different organs and institutions at the enterprise or plant level leads to these conclusions:

1. In practice the employer must deal with trade unions, whether he wishes to or not. He can refuse to recognize a union

delegation in his enterprise and engage in an ensuing struggle, but he is legally obliged to establish a working council and a safety committee in which only union candidates can be elected.

2. The representative trade unions, through their political influence, have succeeded in establishing a shared legal monopoly in the plant or establishment. Only their candidates may appear on the election lists. In some cases, however, unions do not find candidates easily.

3. Leading personnel (i.e., supervisors) do not participate in the elections, nor can they be elected. Since the term "leading personnel" is not clearly defined, many disputes occur between unions and employers and even among the personnel themselves. The fact that leading personnel are not represented as such in the working council has, in my opinion, greatly hampered the unionization of this category of employees.

4. The requirement that the delegate must be elected by all workers, including nonunion personnel, means that sympathetic, but not necessarily competent, people are entered on the lists.

5. In practice the union delegation, working council, and safety committee have overlapping compositions, functions, and jurisdictions. The different structures are not rigidly fixed by law or collective agreement. Working councils and safety and health committees can be reduced to lifeless formalities if they are not supported by strong unions at the plant level. This is true even of the union delegation in many cases.

6. The three organs, especially their union delegations, can be and are the machinery for collective bargaining. The working council has to agree on the work rules and on the scheduling and amounts of annual vacation of employees. But above all—and this differs from industry to industry—many collective agreements are concluded on the level of the enterprise between the employer and the union delegation with the expert aid of the business agents of the different unions involved. This is the case, for example, in the chemical industry, where collective bargaining is done mostly at the plant level.

7. It is fair to draw an overall conclusion that the system is flexible and permits a great deal of constructive freedom

of maneuver, depending on human relations, strength and aggressiveness of unions, and the employers' attitude.

Bargaining Structures at Industry Level: The Joint Committees

Joint committees have played an important role in Belgian labor relations since their inauguration in collective bargaining, the settlement of industrial disputes, and the implementation of social legislation and labor standards. The first joint committees were established on a pragmatic basis in the mining and metal industry after World War I. This number expanded slowly according to union strength and the pace of recognition of unions by associations of employers, which were then also organizing. Only after the economic crisis in the 1930's were a large number of joint committees set up.

In their pact of social solidarity after World War II, employer representatives and trade union representatives expressed their intention to conduct their relations on a basis of mutual respect and reciprocal recognition of each other's rights and duties. They explicitly agreed upon the restoration of the joint committees at the level of the industry. At present, more than 80 such joint committees exist, covering almost all industrial sectors and employers and employees.

It was only after World War II that the joint committees were endowed with a legal status according to the decree of June 9, 1945. This decree was not intended to innovate, but only to confirm the de facto exercise of power and authority of existing institutions by conferring legal status upon them. Essentially, this meant that the committees were and still are built directly upon the trade unions and the employer associations. The new law of December 1968 did not change these features.

Joint committees are established by Royal Decree at the request of, or at least after consultation with, the most representative employer association and trade unions. The Royal Decree defines the territorial and industrial coverage of each committee. Generally, the coverage is the entire industry throughout the nation, but subcommittees are set up which operate under the supervision of the national committee for the particular industry. A single, but multiproduct, enterprise may fall within the scope of several joint committees. In many branches of industry, different committees are set up for manual and white-collar workers, respectively. This is the case in the most important sectors, such as textiles, metals, chemicals, petroleum, and mining.

Joint committees are composed of an equal number of labor and management representatives. These are formally named by the King of Belgium pursuant to actual selection by the Minister of Employment and Labor from the most representative unions and employer associations. As might be expected, there are occasional disputes and displays of pressure regarding the distribution of union designees to joint committees. Each joint committee is staffed by an independent chairman, a vice-chairman, and a secretary of the Ministry of Employment and Labor, in most cases civil servants, also designated by the King.

The joint committees have mainly the following competences: (1) the conclusion of collective labor agreements; (2) a conciliatory mission—to prevent or settle disputes between employers and workers; (3) an advisory mission to advise on problems belonging to the concerned activity. These advices are addressed to the Government, the National Labor Council, the Central Economic Council or the Trades Councils pursuant to the Act of December 1968.

Something has to be said too about the important task of the Department of Employment and Labor in connection with collective labor agreements. First, the Department offers the necessary administrative aid by putting at the disposal of the joint committees the chairman, the secretary, and the indispensable rooms. Second, the collective agreements shall be deposited with the Department of Employment and Labor (Article 18). Before registration, the department exercises a kind of formal supervision over the collective labor agreements in order to determine whether formal instructions have been respected (designation of the parties which conclude the agreements, the duration of the agreement, etc.). The Department delivers, too, on payment of a fee, a copy of the deposited agreement. Third, the intervention of the Department is required when the general binding force is asked (Article 28). This obligation is relative however, the parties not being obliged to ask the general binding force.

The National Labor Council

The National Labor Council, created by the Act of May 29, 1952, had many predecessors. In 1892 a tripartite Supreme Council of Labor was set up. It was composed of representatives of management and labor and specialist-experts. This consultative body played a substantial role in the preparation of a significant number of labor-standards acts voted on by Parliament until 1918.

Taking into account the growing importance of trade unions, the Council was reorganized in 1935 and became more involved in the formulation of social and economic policy. In this prewar period, trade unions and employer associations started significant direct negotiations at the national interindustry level, which culminated in agreements such as the national agreement of 1936 concerning wages, annual vacations, working time, and freedom of trade union activity.

After the war of 1940-45, an informal General Parity Council was created. This council was composed of trade union leaders and employer representatives under the chairmanship of the Minister of Employment and Labor. The General Parity Council prepared a number of important measures requiring implementation or decrees. The program gave expression to the new social ideas and programs that originated even while the war was still a reality. It also concluded nationwide interindustry collective agreements. From the General Parity Council there emerged in 1952 a public body, now called the National Labor Council. The president of the Council is chosen for his economic and social knowledge and independence of trade unions and employer associations. The 22 council members are divided equally between the most representative trade unions and the most representative organizations of employers in industry, agriculture, commerce, and handicraft. The president and members are designated by Royal Decree.

The main function of the Council is to give advice to the legislature or the Executive, on its own initiative or on request, about general social problems concerning employers and workers. In practice the Council has great prestige and is frequently consulted by the Executive. The government would find it very difficult to push a bill on social matters through Parliament if there were serious opposition in the National Labor Council.

The new law of December 5, 1968, gives the National Labor Council the explicit competence to conclude collective labor agreements, while at the same time the former advisory mandate of the Council subsists.

The collective labor agreements in the National Labor Council may belong to two categories: collective labor agreements, covering the entire country and different branches of activity, or covering one particular branch, namely, where for that particular branch a joint committee does not exist or where an established joint committee does not function.

Normally the National Labor Council will occupy itself principally with collective labor agreements of the first category, namely those with a national and interoccupational character. It is difficult to say now if much use of this possibility will be made.

Maybe the employers and workers organizations will in the future prefer the formula of general collective agreements to the intervention of government or Parliament in some fields of labor relations, as, for example, in connection with the working hours. There is also a possibility that the so-called agreements of social programmation, concluded as a rule for a period of two years, would get the formal character of a collective labor agreement in the National Labor Council.

The agreement of social programmation, concluded in the beginning of 1969, provides for instance that a holiday on Saturday has to be replaced by another paid day of rest. It can be imagined that such an agreement would acquire a general legal value by conclusion of a collective labor agreement in the National Labor Council.

It is also possible for the legislator to give the National Labor Council a direct competence to conclude, in fixed matters, collective labor agreements. We know already such an example in the new legislation on contracts of service and salaried employment (Act of November 21, 1969), which provides that the National Labor Council is able to conclude a collective labor agreement, concerning the so-called competition clause, meaning the clause which imposes on the worker some restrictions concerning his employment by another employer.

Collective Bargaining

MAIN FEATURES OF COLLECTIVE BARGAINING

Although collective bargaining may be described as the procedure by which wages and conditions of employment of workers are regulated by agreement between their representatives and employers, the differences in approach, procedure, and scope among different countries are so extensive that a general definition is almost meaningless.

Trade unions in Belgium, and generally employers and employer associations, believe in free collective bargaining without any intervention whatsoever by the government in the establishment of wages and conditions of employment. But the broad statement must be qualified. Through their links with political parties, trade unions have succeeded in pushing through parliament detailed legislation concerning individual labor relations between employer and employee, as well as social security. Many questions that are the subject of collective bargaining in the United States are governed by law in Belgium. Acts concerning individual labor contracts for blue-collar and white-collar workers regulate, among other things, different forms of contracts, damages for breach thereof, layoff, period of notice prior to dismissal, illness, working time, overtime, female and child labor, safety and working conditions, holidays with pay, paid annual leaves, and the like. There are also very detailed social security regulations dealing with unemployment, sickness and health insurance, pensions, occupational diseases, and family allowances.

With so much social and labor legislation, there is, of course, less room for collective bargaining. The process of private bargaining must take into account the existing legal rules. While these are mostly protective minimum standards that could be improved by collective bargaining, nevertheless collective bargaining does not cover as many items as a system with fewer legal restrictions. Many agreements on the national level concern only wages, premium pay for night, dangerous, or unpleasant work, and job classifications for individual employees. In some sectors of the economy, especially the expanding ones, agreements might stipulate other items, but legally they build upon some existing legal provisions. The petroleum sector, for example, is covered by different national agreements which cover the following items for blue-collar workers: (1) job classification, (2) working time, (3) wages, premiums, and cost-of-living clause, (4) overtime, (5) absence with pay (civic and other obligations), (6) vacation (legal vacation), (7) additional pension, (8) sickness indemnity (improvement of legal system), (9) job stability (improvement of legal system), and (10) grievance procedure (union delegation). From items (4) through (9) the collective agreement provides some improvements over existing legal benefits not dependent on the agreement.

The large financial commitments to social security and other social benefits, namely more than 50 percent of gross wages for blue-collar workers and more than 40 percent for white-collar workers, inevitably affect the collective bargaining process. Indeed, these percentages of wages receive a legal destination that cannot be modified by collective bargaining. While the government does not formally intervene in the setting of wages and benefits, it intervenes indirectly by fixing the social security contributions and compels the parties to bargain within a limited scope.

STAFF PERSONNEL AND COLLECTIVE BARGAINING

Staff personnel or cadre employees are not involved in collective bargaining. This is not so much the consequence of the absence of bargaining machinery, since the joint committees for white-collar workers may represent all white-collar employees. But an examination of collective agreements concluded in joint committees shows clearly that in almost all cases wages and employment conditions of supervisory personnel above the level of foreman are omitted. It is also established that at the enterprise level the union delegation does not include representatives of cadre or leading personnel. The main reason is that leading personnel either are not unionized or do not affiliate with the representative trade union. Accordingly, individual contracts or, more likely, unilateral employer determination establishes the wage and labor conditions of staff personnel.

NATIONAL INTERINDUSTRY BARGAINING

Before World War II, there began the practice of concluding nationwide interindustry agreements. This practice was continued and even expanded after the war. More than 30 such agreements were concluded. These agreements were, of course, not all of equal importance, but some have really influenced the overall picture of labor relations in the postwar period up to now. An example is the aforementioned pact of social solidarity by which the employers and labor representatives expressed their willingness to cooperate loyally and constructively. The pact contained a number of principles and stipulated the renewal of the joint committees, the idea of the union delegation and similar matters.

Another important interindustry agreement, which has been in force since 1947, concerns the institution and working of the union delegation. Since 1958, interindustry agreements have also dealt with supplementary holidays, productivity, and the working council.

An unusual interindustry agreement is the "Pact of Social Programation," which was concluded on May 11, 1960. Trade unions and employer associations laid down three fundamental principles:

1. A concerted policy of economic expansion must enable workers to share in a regularly improving standard of living.

2. This participation of the workers in the improvement of their standard of living must be realized through collective agreements, concluded at national interindustry level, by which the share of workers in the growth of the national wealth is programmed for a fixed period. National agreements by industry sector and agreements at the plant level must program supple-

mentary advantages. The programmation will, however, take into account governmental social security benefits, financed through employer contributions.

3. This programmation is possible only if industrial peace is observed during the life of the collective agreements. Social programmation dealt specifically with family allowances and annual vacation. Further agreements, concluded in the same spirit in 1963 and 1966, stipulated the third week of annual vacation at double pay. Negotiation at the national industry-wide level since 1960 has been incorporated into social programmation.

INDUSTRY-WIDE BARGAINING

Most industrial sectors are covered by national agreements. These national agreements assume varying documentary forms. In some sectors, such as the chemical industry, they will be almost meaningless, since the major collective bargaining is done in that sector at the plant or establishment level. In the construction, petroleum, textile, and metal industries, the national agreements are more elaborate. Nevertheless, national agreements generally leave room for matters to be determined at the level of the enterprise. They are "minimum agreements" which can be improved. Statistics show differences in wages, according to regions, plant size, or other factors.

In some national agreements, in the textile and metal industries for example, the national trade unions have agreed that no general claims should be made at the level of the enterprise. This means that the national agreement is in principle final. But many companies that pay "better wages" or want to attract labor may permissibly pay above the national scale.

In the metal industry important changes in collective bargaining for blue-collar workers have occurred since the programmation idea started in 1960. Before 1960, the metal industry was characterized by traditional union activity in an atmosphere of struggle and strong employer opposition to unions. Union claims were supported primarily by means of strikes or threats to strike. Union activity was for the most part concentrated at the plant level. Where the workers were sufficiently organized, advantages were extorted "with the fist." The chief aim of programmation was to generalize through national agreements the benefits that had been obtained only in some enterprises. The activity of the different joint committees was of course very limited. Nevertheless, national agreements were reached on certain matters, namely, the union delegation, cost-of-living clause, absence with pay for civic or family obligations, and a 45-hour work week. No national agreement was reached on wages.

In 1960 the programmation on the national level started in the steel industry as well as in the metalworking industry. Following social programmation, agreements were achieved in the metalworking industry for varying periods from August 1960 to December 1963. In 1964 no national agreement was concluded, bargaining occurring mainly at the establishment level. But two-year national agreements were made for the calendar years of 1965 and 1966 and for the calendar years of 1967 and 1968.

The national agreements in steel and metal industry cover wages and benefits and working time, among other things. Except for the year 1964, essential bargaining since 1960 has been concluded at the national level. The national agreements contain an explicit statement that no claim of a general or collective nature may be made by the trade union at the level of the enterprise. This clause, however, does not exclude individual wage adjustments for age, security, or personal merits, changes in a wage structure resulting from a change in the organization of work, or restudy of unusual and significant wage cases.

In return for the social programmation, employers get "social peace" during the life of the agreements. This means that trade unions accept as their responsibility the enormous task of safeguarding social peace during the fixed agreement period. According to the peace obligation, trade unions are required to prevent wildcat or unofficial strikes and to get the workers back to work should one occur. If workers continue to strike, trade unions may not award strike benefits to strikers. In return for safeguarding social peace, trade unions receive from the employer, through the employer association, which collects the money, a financial "subvention" of 0.5 percent of gross wages. If the trade unions support striking employees, the subvention is diminished by an amount equal to $2.50 daily for each striking employee. The reduction becomes an amount equal to $5.00 daily per striker if the strike continues for more than 20 days.

Social programmation is a recent phenomenon in labor management relations. It is difficult to foresee whether it will continue to develop smoothly in the future. Much will depend on the approach and attitudes of the involved parties and on practical experience.

Solution of two problems will largely determine whether the system will continue. One problem is raised by management and the other by labor. The problem that concerns management is union insistence upon cost-of-living clauses. The automatic adaptation of wages to rises in the cost of living was long ago obtained by trade unions. In the system of social programmation, cost-of-living adjustments are being resisted by the employers. The employers' argument is that since programmation fixes social burdens, its meaning is lost if wages must be adjusted every time there is a rise in the cost of living. Another uncertainty within the system is, of course, the likely rise of social security contributions, upon which government may decide unilaterally.

The problem unions face is union activity at the plant or enterprise level. Social programmation at the national level means the setting of wages and labor conditions on the basis of the potential and possibilities of the "average' 'enterprise. Consequently, in theory at least, all enterprises should bear the same burdens. From labor's point of view, there is fear that the rules fixed at the national level will become too rigid and especially that wages will not be able to be adjusted upward in accordance with special regional or plant circumstances. Unions feel that national agreements do not take into account the discrepancy between prosperous and less well-to-do enterprises. Consequently, trade unions propose more flexibility in the programmation and the possibility of bargaining on some matters at the enterprise level.

BARGAINING AT THE LEVEL OF THE ENTERPRISE

Although programmation on the national level may have resulted in a general reduction of the bargaining activity at the plant level, many individual establishment collective agreements are still concluded. National agreements do not cover all terms, and there are minima which can and should be improved. In many industries, of which the chemical industry is a prime example, the real bargaining is done at the enterprise level, and bargaining at the national level is insignificant.

Experienced Belgian employers are wary of reaching an agreement with only one of the trade unions even if that union has organized a large majority of the workers in the establishment. The other union will not accept exclusion and will not rest until it has been recognized as full spokesman. As a rule, it is better for employers to avoid interfering in trade union competition and to accept negotiations only on common proposals. However, employers are more inclined to fall into line with the program urged by the strongest trade union. This applies equally when negotiations are undertaken on the level of industry.

Since collective agreements establish only minimum standards, an employer might be compelled to afford better conditions to attract workers. He may respond similarly if the plant traditionally has been a high-wage establishment or the undertaking is situated in a highly industrialized, high-wage region. In such cases there is considerable individual bargaining or "workplace" bargaining, with small groups within the enterprise.

Collective Bargaining and the Law of December 5, 1968

The new law of 1968 did not change these patterns and features. However, it contains some fundamental options, which are of the greatest importance for the future of collective bargaining. The right to conclude collective agreements in the sense of the law, is exclusively reserved to the most representative trade unions.

The new law foresees that the delegates of the organizations shall be presumed to have the competence to conclude an agreement on behalf of their organization. The ruling is irrefutable

(Article 12). However, nowhere is it clearly stated who is a delegate of the organization, and which procedure indicates that he is recognized as such. The same Article 12 has also a consequence that the agreement is legally binding even if the employees-members reject it.

The trade unions and employers associations, even lacking legal personality, are given the capacity to sue and be sued (1) in all litigation arising out of this act, (2) to defend their members' rights arising out of the agreements concluded by them.

Here there is an important innovation. The trade union, for example, can sue de jure on behalf of its members even without the permission or the consent of the individual worker. The reason for this is that the individual employee might himself be afraid to sue or to give his union a mandate to do so. Thus, in principle, it is possible that the union could sue the employer on behalf of an individual employee-member, even against the consent of the individual employee. However, the individual member is not allowed to sue his union. In my opinion, the union has to prove the membership of the employee, although some other writers disagree. The union does not even have an obligation to reveal the employee's name.

Most important, however, is that "damages for nonperformance of the obligations arising out of an agreement may be claimed from organizations only in so far as the agreement expressly provides for this" (Article 4). This means that a trade union cannot be sued for a claim for damages if it called for a strike regardless of a peace obligation. It is only in so far as the collective agreement itself provides for a remedy that some action is possible.

The new law also foresees that the collective agreements must be written containing specific information concerning parties, duration, etc. which are to be deposited with the Ministry of Employment and Labor. As such, collective agreements will have (especially at the level of the undertaking), the form of informal understandings, memos, and the like. There will be more opportunities for all involved to know what is going on, if it is possible to obtain a copy of the agreements.

As far as the parties competent to conclude a collective agreement are concerned, a distinction has to be made between workers and employers. Only trade unions are competent to make this distinction for workers, whereas for the employers both organizations and individual employers can be party to a collective agreement (Article 5). Both for workers' and for employers' organizations, the condition is that those organizations would be representative. The law itself provides the criteria of representation (Article 3).

For the workers' organizations, the law dictates four conditions: that they have an interoccupational character; that they be established at the national level; that they be represented on the Central Economic Council and the National Labor Council; and that they have at least 50,000 members. Actually, this means that only the following organizations are considered to be representative: the Confédération des Syndicats Chrétiens, the Fédération Générale du Travail de Belgique, and the Centrale Générale des Syndicats Libéraux de Belgique. This recognition covers the organizations affiliated to or belonging to one of the three organizations, for example, a trade union center, as the Center of Metalworkers affiliated to the FGTB is considered as a representative organization which is able to conclude collective labor agreements.

In the discussions in Parliament and by some authors, this legal provision has been criticized because of the privileged status it gives to some organizations. If, for example, in a certain industrial branch or factory a trade union disposes of the majority of workers, but is not affiliated to one of the three national confederations, this trade union would not be able to conclude a collective agreement, at least an agreement with a juridical value. It would at most be able to make a convention with a moral significance.

The following representative employer organizations are recognized as representative (Article 3):

1. The employer organizations with a national and interoccupational character and represented on the Central Economic Council and the National Labor Council. Consequently, three

of the four criteria are the same as for the workers' organizations. The fourth criterion, the number of members, has not been taken into consideration.

2. The employer organizations, nonaffiliated to the above-mentioned employer organizations, but which in any given branch of activity are declared to be representative by the Crown. Indeed, some employers' organizations are not affiliated to an interoccupational organization, as the Federation of Belgian Industry. This is the case in the transport sector. However, a Royal Order would be necessary to recognize such associations after the advice of the National Labor Council.

3. The middle-class organizations are considered as representative under the act of March 6, 1964. Actually, the following organizations are represented in the Central Economic Council and the National Labor Council: the Federation of Belgian Industry; the Federation of Belgian Nonindustrial Undertakings; two agricultural organizations, the Belgische Boerenbond and the Fédération Nationale des Unions Professionnelles Agricoles; the Middle-Class Organization; the Flemish Economic Association.

The agricultural organizations, however, are not interoccupational organizations; consequently a Royal Order will be necessary to recognize these organizations as representative.

The Act provides that collective agreements may be made within a joint body or outside. Taking into consideration the existing practice, we may suppose that in the future the collective agreements will be made mostly within a joint body. The legal value of these agreements is indeed larger than the value of the agreements concluded outside a joint body. According to the law there are three kinds of joint bodies: the National Labor Council, the joint committees, and the joint subcommittees (Article 1).

In the content of the collective agreements, distinctions should be made between the formal and conventional contents. The formal content concerns a number of formal rules, which have to be observed in order to make the collective labor agreement valid in law. This is regulated by Articles 13 to 16 of the Act of 1968.

The agreement has to be made in writing and must contain a number of items such as the names of the organizations concluding the agreement, the name of the joint body on which the agreement is concluded, the scope of application of the collective labor agreement, the duration of validity or the modes of termination and the periods of termination, etc. As already noted, the deposit of the collective agreement will not be accepted by the Department of Employment and Labor if the agreement fails to fulfil these formal instructions (Article 18).

The conventional content of the collective agreement can be divided in two parts: the so-called obligatory stipulations and the normative stipulations. The obligatory stipulations concern the rights and duties of the parties concluding a collective agreement; the normative stipulations concern the relation between employers and workers.

Obligatory stipulations are indicated in Article 5 of the Act dealing with "the rights and obligations of the contracting parties." The Act itself does not stipulate these rights and obligations. Consequently, the collective agreement itself has to stipulate these obligations.

It is generally admitted, however, especially under influence of the German jurisprudence, that some obligatory stipulations belong to the essence of the collective agreements, although they are not explicitly mentioned in the agreement. Such is the case with the so-called peace obligation. By peace obligation we mean that the parties concluding a collective agreement have to abstain from lock-out or strike, so long as the collective agreement is in force. This peace obligation is relative however, unless the parties provide otherwise. This means that lock-out and strike are only to be considered as breach of contract when they are related to matters ruled by the collective agreement. If, for example, a collective agreement fixes only wages, a strike with the intention to get an extension of the competence of the work councils would not mean a breach of contract.

We have to stress again the fact that violations of the peace obligations can not lead to juridical claims unless explicitly mentioned by the parties. This results from Article 4 which provides only indemnification for nonperformance of the obligation in so far as the agreement expressly provides for this. In the actual state of Belgian law, the peace obligation is thus a moral and not a legal engagement.

In regard to normative stipulations, a distinction is to be made between individual and collective normative stipulations (Article 5). Individual stipulations contain rules, covering individual contracts. The collective stipulations, on the contrary, order the collective relations in the enterprises or in the branch of activity. Stipulations concerning wages, holidays, work hours, etc., belong to the first group.

Examples of collective stipulations are: stipulations, ruling the order in which eventual collective dismissals will take place; stipulations in relation to the social welfare services in the factory, etc. This distinction is not merely academic; it has practical consequences, since the collective normative stipulations have a lesser legal value than the individual (cf. Article 26).

Until the law of December 5, 1968, the Belgium legal framework did not provide a *specific* regulation as to the status of the collective agreement. The 1968 Act provides a specific and exhaustive regulation of the status of collective agreements. The collective agreement is recognized as a valid legal instrument.

Article 19 provides that the collective agreement is binding on: (1) the organizations which concluded it and the employers who are members of such organizations which have considered the agreement, as from the date of its coming into force; (2) the organizations and employers subsequently acceding to the agreement, and the employers' members of such organizations, as from the date of their accession; (3) employers who become affiliated with an organization, bound by the agreement, as from the date of their affiliation; (4) all the workers in the service of an employer bound by the agreement.

As to the *employees,* all employees, even the nonunionized, employed by an employer otherwise bound by the agreement have the benefit of the provisions of the agreement.

The binding effect of the agreement as it concerns the *employer* depends in principle upon his being a member of the organization which concluded the agreement (this includes, of course, the case where the employer himself concluded the agreement). To the basic question of how to ascertain whether an employer is a member or not of a particular organization, the law does not provide a specific answer.

Under the Act of December 1968 an employers' association cannot be forced to declare which are its members, nor could an individual employer be obligated to communicate to which association or organization he belongs. The working solution at the moment in case of dispute or controversy is an engagement of the national interprofessional employers' organizations in the National Labor Council to communicate the membership information to the unions, whenever such will be requested. Whether this will be effective in practice remains to be seen. Meanwhile it can be expected that problems will arise, mainly concerning little enterprises!

The binding effect of the collective agreement is furthermore extended by law to other employers than those contractually bound. Article 26 provides that the clauses of an agreement which deal with *individual relations* between employers and employees shall be binding on *employers* not affiliated with a signatory organization but covered by the joint committee within which the agreement is concluded.

The principle of supplementary binding effect of the individual normative provisions of a collective agreement depends on four conditions to be performed: (1) the collective agreement must be concluded in a joint body; (2) employers and employees must be covered by the competence of the joint body; (3) employers and employees must fall within the scope of the agreement; (4) the individual contract of employment contains no written clause contrary to the provision of the collective agreement in question.

A few remarks should be made as to these four conditions. "Concluded within a joint body" refers (see Article 1 of the Act) to agreements concluded within the National Labor Council, the joint committees or joint subcommittees.

Furthermore, "joint body" does not cover the works council. The binding effect of the so-called enterprise agreements is regulated by Article 19. The employer will be bound as

37

signatory party of the agreement. In general, an agreement on the level of the enterprise will be concluded through the union delegation, eventually with the assistance of the union business agent.

Employers and employees must fall within the competence of the joint body. Agreements concluded in the National Labor Council cover in principle all branches of activity throughout the entire country (Article 7, par. 1) except when it takes over the function of a nonworking joint committee. The competence of the joint committee and subcommittee is determined by the King after previous consultation of the professional organizations (Articles 35, 36).

Parties must be covered by the scope of application of the agreement. As an important application of the "contractual" concept of the collective agreement, parties are free to determine this scope of application. Consequently, the parties may exclude from its scope some categories of employers or employees, a given territory, a given activity, or certain enterprises. The scope of application of the agreement should thus be carefully checked out.

Article 26 provides for a formalized deviation procedure: the nonaffiliated employer may stipulate provisions contrary to the collective agreement by an individually written clause of the individual contract of employment.

The twofold requirement of an *individual* and *written* clause is an expressly provided guarantee for the employee. But the nonapplication of Article 26 can result from every sufficiently precise clause, if written and individual, even if such a clause was inserted in the contract of employment before the existence of the collective agreement. Thus, a general clause in vague terms will not be accepted for such purpose ("sufficiently precise" being essential), but it is not required that after the conclusion of a collective agreement that all individual contracts of employment must be corrected. It can be previously done if "sufficiently precise." Nevertheless, it seems to be quite difficult in practice to preview forthcoming situations covered by the collective agreement in "sufficiently precise" terms.

The scope of application of Article 26 is further limited by the fact that it concerns only the clauses which deal with the individual relations between employers and employees.

This binding effect upon the nonorganized employer will come into force fifteen days after the publication in the *Moniteur Belge (Belgisch Staatsblad)* of the notice; it has to mention the object, date, duration, scope, and place of deposit of the collective agreement. This is to allow the nonorganized employer to inform himself of the contract, for example by obtaining a copy of the agreement as provided for by Article 18.

The binding effect of the agreement can be even further extended, through the technique of a Royal Order declaring an agreement to be generally binding. In such a case Article 31 provides that an agreement rendered generally binding shall bind all the employers and workers falling within the jurisdiction of the joint body and within the scope of the agreement. This binding effect covers *all* normative provisions, i.e., the clauses dealing with the individual relationship as well as the clauses dealing with the collective relations between employers and their employees.

No deviation procedure is provided for in such cases; in fact penal sanctions are set forward (Article 56, 1) in the event of nonapplication of the agreement concerned.

To summarize: the binding effect of the collective agreement could be classified in three stages:

1. The collective agreement in general is binding on all contracting and organized employers and employees (Article 19); the agreement shall be deposited with the Ministry of Employment and Labor, and any person may obtain a copy of the agreement (Article 18).

2. The collective agreements concluded in a joint body have only a supplementary binding effect for nonorganized employers and their employees (Article 26), and are published by notice inserted in the *Moniteur Belge* (Article 25).

3. The collective agreements rendered generally binding by Royal Order are binding on all covered employers (Article 31)

and are published in the *Moniteur Belge* as annex to the Royal Order (Article 30).

Article 51 establishes a list of the legal sources in a hierarchical order which regulates the individual relation:

The sources of the obligations arising out of the employment relation between employers and workers shall be as follows, in descending order of precedence:

1. the law in its peremptory provisions;
2. collective industrial agreements declared to be generally binding, in the following order:
    (a) agreements concluded in the National Labor Council;
    (b) agreements concluded in a joint committee;
    (c) agreements concluded in a joint subcommittee;
3. collective industrial agreements which have not been declared to be generally binding, where the employer is a signatory thereto or is affiliated to an organization signatory to such agreement, in the following order:
    (a) agreements concluded in the National Labor Council;
    (b) agreements concluded in a joint committee;
    (c) agreements concluded in a joint subcommittee;
    (d) agreements concluded outside a joint body;
4. an individual agreement in writing;
5. a collective industrial agreement concluded in a joint body but not declared generally binding, where the employer, although not a signatory thereto or not affiliated to an organization signatory thereto, is within the jurisdiction of the joint body in which the agreement was concluded;
6. work rules;
7. the supplementary provisions of the law;
8. a verbal individual agreement;
9. custom.

·II·

The Civil Service

IN Belgium the setting of wages and working conditions of the public employee belongs in principle to the discretionary competence of the government (national, provincial, or local) which acts *unilaterally* by way of "statute." Wages and working conditions, in general, are to be regulated in the interest of the public service and can be changed unilaterally following the needs of the public service (bonum commune). Legally, collective bargaining in the public sector aimed at reaching an enforceable agreement is an impossibility except to some extent in proprietary enterprises. There is legally only room for an advisory function on the part of the trade unions or the representatives of the personnel. In practice however, wages and working conditions are set by formally negotiated and signed collective agreements, labeled as such, but which for the reason of enforceability have to be put into effect through law or government regulations.

Public employment is heavily influenced by *politics*. Jobs and assignments are divided following party lines, and the fact that the three main trade unions have, as indicated above, close links with the political parties, is of the greatest significance.[1] This certainly affects heavily the degree of unionization—as appointment or promotion may depend on political or on trade union backing. It greatly influences labor relations, as the heads of departments will, for practical reasons, discuss and bargain only with their trade union friends. This in turn has favored patterns which reserve trade union action for the so-called representative trade unions.

Another main feature of labor relations in the public sector is undoubtedly the de facto centralization by the national government of wages and working conditions, which will be discussed

1. Undoubtedly, given the great number of public employees as a voting force, political parties and cabinet officers attach a great deal of importance to the status of public employees in handling their problems, and in campaigns. These matters are, however, part of the general program of political parties in promoting the interests of the workers in general.

later in more detail. However, one consequence can already be indicated: the setting of general wages and labor conditions by the national government means that trade union activity is mainly centered at the national level and underlines the unique importance of the "social programmation agreements," which covers all workers of the public sector in its broadest sense, as well as those who are already on pension.

The capital influence of the cabinet system cannot be stressed enough. The fact that the government relies on a majority within Parliament[2] means that agreements made by government, will as a general rule be implemented by Parliament as far as the necessary budgetary implications are concerned.

Although most of the aforementioned characteristics prevail in government controlled agencies, whose activities are closely linked or comparable to private industry and commerce, such as railroads, airways, tramways, buses and related activities, important differences with the public service in general can be noted especially as far as labor relations are concerned. In the railroads, collective bargaining has been legally set up since 1926, while Sabena Airlines (National Airlines) and tramways and buses[3] have the bargaining structure which prevails in the private sector. In Sabena, tramways and buses, union delegations are active, and working councils and joint committees have been established.[4] For teachers in the private sector,[5] collective bargaining is also conducted through joint committees. All this will be discussed later in more detail.

Finally, it should be said that often it is claimed that wages and benefits in the public sector lag behind those of the private sector, but that the public sector is moving quickly toward filling the gap, especially as far as lower ranking employees are concerned. The public sector, however, has still two great advan-

2. The same is true for the municipal council and the provincial council, as far as the municipal and provincial budgets are concerned.
3. See further, Chapter IV.
4. For the role and function of union delegation, working council, health and safety committee and joint committee see Chapter I.
5. Teachers of private schools are included in the discussion of public employee unionism because the government regulates almost all working and labor conditions for such teachers. In consequence, the teacher organizations negotiate principally with the government.

tages compared with the private sector: (1) almost complete job security, which still attracts many people; (2) an excellent pension system. A civil servant can only be dismissed in exceptional circumstances such as absence without justification for more than 10 days or the commitment of a crime involving a juridical condemnation to forced labor or other severe sanction. In the private sector, on the other hand, an employee can be dismissed, even without reason, given the appropriate period of notice.

The Public Sector Labor Force

Public employment in Belgium is in constant growth and in 1968 comprised 531,110 persons, which is about 15 percent of the total active population. For 1967 employment in the main public services was as follows: departments (national civil servants): 106,069; provinces: 6,247; municipalities, including public safety employees—police, firemen, and the like: 62,544; public assistance,[6] including health employees: 22,330; army: 57,732; national guard (gendarmerie): 12,479; magistrates: 4,444; teachers—public: 40,031; teachers—private (mainly Catholic): 96,000; railways: 57,912; postal office: 22,653; Sabena Airlines: 10,355.[7]

Collective Bargaining Developments—Social Programmation

Collective bargaining on a national level, including the public sector as a whole, developed fully in the 1960's. Since that time other subsequent agreements have been concluded. A first agreement concluded July 1, 1962, covered the years 1962, 1963, and 1964. The second agreement was a one-year agreement for the year 1965. The third agreement for 1966-67 was for the first time formally signed by the trade unions, the Prime Minister, the Vice-Prime Minister, and other cabinet officers. The fourth agreement covered the years 1968-69, while the last agreement covers the years 1970-71. The subject matter

6. Organized at muncipality level and in charge of most public hospitals.
7. Bijlagen VIII en V van het verslag van de werkgroep bij de 4e sociale programmatie.

of those collective agreements was mainly wages, fringe benefits (vacation pay), pensions, social security, work accidents, working time, benefits of vacation and trade union-government relations. Different (sectorial) collective agreements are concluded in airlines, tramways and busses, railroads and other decentralized national agencies, covering a wide range of wages and labor conditions.

In addition to these agreements, trade unions play an important and often effective role through consultation machinery which is set up, which will be discussed later. One may state that collective bargaining in the public sector, although on the whole still relatively new, has become well-established and has for the last ten years worked well in the different sectors, where it has been introduced. In those sectors it can be labeled as mature. One can predict with almost complete certainty that collective bargaining in the public sector will even become more and more important in the years ahead.

·III·

Trade Unions and the Public Employer

THE RIGHT TO ORGANIZE

WITH the exception of the army and the national guard, which constitute a special problem,[1] public employees have an express right to organize. They benefit from the Act of May 24, 1921, which guarantees freedom of association. According to Article 1 of this Act, "no person shall be compelled to join or refrain from joining any association." Union security clauses such as closed shop, union shop, agency shop, and maintenance of membership are unknown in the public sector. Belgian labor law does not provide for any specific legal obligation to bargain with unions of public employees. However, trade unions are so much a fact of life that bargaining with them is self-evident.

Most public employees are organized in the two big trade unions, the Socialist and the Christian unions. Following their own indications, both organizations have an equal strength and organize respectively 33 to 34 percent of employees eligible for membership. All the other organizations together claim to group from 10 to 12 percent of the public employees. As such, almost 80 percent of persons eligible for trade union membership are affiliated. These figures are very tentative and, as indicated, rely on trade union sources. Although it may be somewhat exaggerated, the two largest trade unions, as a result of their great influence in public employment, are likely to attract a great number of workers.

TRADE UNION STRUCTURE

The Federation of Christian Trade Unions of the Public Ser-

1. Military personnel and national guards (gendarmes) have their own organizations, which are more of the friendly associations type than real trade unions. They operate under firm control of the army and the national guard. In 1963 a trade union for gendarmes was created, but its action was swiftly put to an end by drastic government intervention. Gendarmes who refused to give up their membership were dismissed.

vices groups six trade unions and coordinates their activities. The most important is undoubtedly the Christian Trade Union of Public Services (CCOD), which had 57,006 members in 1967. The CCOD is subdivided into different groups, each group corresponding to certain administrative agencies. The different groups are as follows:

1. State: all departments, with the exception of Finance and Transport;
2. Finance: Department of Finance;
3. Decentralized agencies: with the exception of corporations of mixed economy and those depending on the Department of Transport;
4. Province, municipalities: including public assistance;
5. Tramways and buses;
6. Airlines.

The second trade union is the Christian Union of Railway, Post and Telephone Offices, Shipping, Civil Aviation, Radio and Television Workers. It organizes 36,015 employees. The four other trade unions concern teachers: teachers in primary schools (46,322 members); teachers in public high schools (2,748 members); teachers in free high schools (8,102 members), and teachers in technical schools (20,398). The fact that there are four teacher unions is due mainly to historical reasons; many believe these should be a single union.

The Socialist trade unions are composed of different national sections, namely departments, gas and electricity, education, decentralized agencies, postal workers, radio and television, railroads, tramways and buses, provinces and municipalities, and telegraphy and telephone, which are more or less independent as far as bargaining and consultations are concerned.

As indicated before, the Socialist (General Federation of Public Services) and Christian (Federation of Christian Trade Unions of the Public Services) unions are affiliated respectively with the FGTB and the CSC. The Liberal Union is part of the centralized Liberal Trade Unions.[2] The "Independent

2. The position of the Liberal unions in the public sector is not quite clear. One segment is affiliated with the Liberal Trade Unions, another acts independently and relies on the Political Party of Liberty and Progress.

Trade Unions," which are a conglomerate of smaller trade unions within the public services, have no counterpart in the private sector. Other groups or associations that have relatively little or no importance, like the National Police Association, have of course no relations with private sector unions.

The fact that the main trade unions belong to larger federations undoubtedly affects their strength both financially as well as politically, and certainly at the bargaining table. For example, the Christian Trade Union of Public Services can rely, if need be, on a central strike fund to which the whole Christian trade union movement contributes. However, each national trade union within the federation is autonomous in defending the interest of its members, and affiliation with the CSC or the FGTB certainly does not affect bargaining objectives to a great extent. It should be noted that for many years the Christian and Socialist Trade Unions in the public sector acted in a "common front" which meant that they bargained together with the government or other agencies.

Trade union action and management—trade union relations in the private sector have influenced trade unionism in the public sector and will undoubtedly continue to do so. The bargaining set-up and models of the "joint committees" which operate successfully in the private sector are looked upon, both by government officials as well as trade unionists, as the example to be fully introduced in the public sector.

RECOGNITION OF TRADE UNIONS

Recognition of trade unions in the public sector is not at all uniformly regulated. Two main patterns can, however, be observed: the first one is characterized by a great facility in obtaining recognition, and regulated by the Royal Decree of 1955; the second, which will soon become the dominant pattern, restricts recognition to the most representative trade unions. This last model operates among others within the Railroads.

Theoretically, the Royal Decree of June 20, 1955, is still the only legal basis authorizing trade union action for an important part of the public sector. The Royal Decree applies mainly to the public employees of the national departments, the decentralized national agencies, and teachers in public state schools. It does not apply to Sabena, railroads, tramways and buses, municipalities, provinces, or public assistances where other (or no) rules are in effect.

The Royal Decree permits two kinds of recognition:

1. The particular recognition for a specific department or a specific public service. This recognition can be easily obtained. No elections are involved. The only requirements are that the trade union, which seeks to defend the. interests of all or part of the employees of the given department or public service, send by registered post a request for recognition together with a copy of bylaws and the list of the leaders of the organization to the competent cabinet officer or board of governors.

2. General recognition to all departments and public services, within the scope of the Royal Decree, can be obtained by the trade unions which are already recognized by one department and have obtained seats in the general trade union advisory council or are represented in the National Labor Council. These unions must forward by registered post a copy of their bylaws and the list of their leaders to the Prime Minister.

The recognized trade unions have several rights: first, they can intervene with the competent authorities by which they are recognized in defense of the interests of the employees as a group or for the benefit of an individual employee. This does not mean that unions enjoy the right to bargain; they merely have the right to express their point of view. Second, they can organize meetings on the premises with the permission of the competent authority and to use posters (bulletins of the public service boards, and the like).

The most representative trade unions complain bitterly about the case in which recognition, especially the specific recognition, can be obtained. Four organizations obtained general recognition; many more obtained specific recognition: department of transport—30 organizations; department of finance—17 organizations; department of defense—14 organizations, and so on.

Essentially, the Socialist and Christian trade unions want to eliminate the smaller groups and to establish a monopoly for trade union action in the public sector of the same format as in the private sector. Along these lines the national collective agreement of January 26, 1968, foresees expressly that the government will drastically change trade union relations within the public sector, taking into account the following principles:

1. That the government respect trade union freedom.

2. That the government adequately and usefully bargain only with the most representative unions, to the exclusion of all others. The government is convinced that it does not curtail trade union freedom if it negotiates only with trade unions capable of bearing responsibilities on a national level.

3. That the selection of most representative unions occurs following strict objective criteria.

4. That the new regulations on trade union relations in the public sector must also permit the establishment of organs capable of promoting human relations and productivity.

This agreement, which has been reaffirmed in the latest national collective agreement of July 29, 1969, will, as such, establish a legal and practical monopoly for the two big unions by representing the interests of the workers at all levels of the public sector.

Railroads: Setting the New Pattern

The situation as it exists now in the railroads—the National Corporation of Belgian Railroads operated under the Minister for Transport as a corporation with the government as its chief shareholder—is of extreme importance as a pacesetter for the trade union objectives in the public sector, insofar as recognition and bargaining is concerned. The activity of trade unions in the NCBR is based on the Act of July 23, 1926, by which the corporation was established. The most representative unions have two representatives on the board of directors, who govern the corporation. Article 13 of the 1926 Act provides for the creation of a national joint committee. The principal duty of the committee is to establish the "statutes" of the employees, such as wages and working conditions. The national joint committee is composed of 10 representatives of the corporation, appointed by the board of governors of the corporation and 10 representatives of the trade unions. Over this last representation a long and difficult battle was fought, out of which the most representative, in this case the Christian and Socialist unions, emerged with the help of Parliament as victors.

In 1962 the board of governors changed the rules toward representation in the joint committee and stated that trade unions in order to be recognized and take seats in the joint committee should be affiliated with a national interindustry-wide federation of trade unions, which organizes at least 50,000 members and is represented in the National Labor Council. One of the consequences of these changes was the elimination of the Independent Trade Union of Public Services. The Council of State[3] declared the decision of the board of governors void on the grounds that neither the law of 1926 nor the law of 1952 on the National Labor Council could offer reasonable legal grounds to justify the decision of 1962. Thereupon the Belgian Parliament changed Article 13 of the Act of 1926 on April 21, 1965, and set new criteria in order to determine the representative unions: trade union representatives would be appointed by organizations which were most representative as well internally within the corporation as on national and industry-wide level. The new act left it to the joint committee of NCBR itself to work their criteria out into practical rules. The new rules are: (1) accept as members all the employees of the NCBR; (2) be affiliated with a national and interindustry-wide trade union which groups at least 50,000 members and is represented in the National Labor Council; (3) organize at least 10 percent of the total work force of the NCBR.[4]

3. "Arrêt" of November 28, 1963. *Winand* vs. *NCBR*. The Council of State is the highest court regarding administrative matters.

4. See also *Bulletin Officiel*, B.I.T., January 1967, case number 281. *Rapports du Comité de la liberté syndicale institué par le Conseil d'administration*, pp. 12-15. The independent union had introduced a complaint that the situation in the NCBR was in contradiction with ILO conventions on trade union freedom. In vague language, the Committee for Trade Union Freedom states that the fact that a member not be seated in the joint committee did not of necessity imply that there was an infringement of trade union freedom, if (1) the elimination was based on the lack of representation, determined by objective criteria, and (2) that

As such, the Socialist and Christian trade unions got what they wanted: exclusive representation for themselves within the joint committee. Moreover, only those two organizations are recognized and are allowed to intervene directly with the administration to defend the interests of their members. Individual grievances can be introduced by the individual himself or by the recognized trade unions. There is little possibility of action left for nonrecognized trade unions. An individual can in the processing of his grievance be assisted by another employee, who could be an official of a nonrecognized union. But this intervention would be in his capacity as another employee, not in his official capacity as the nonrecognized trade union representative. It is not surprising that the labor relations within the railroads, where the most representative trade unions are said to exist, have eliminated competitors and have realized for many years real collective bargaining through the national joint committee, which are looked upon by the trade unions as the goals to be achieved in the public sector as a whole. Undoubtedly the pattern set by the railroads will be the determining one for the future outlook of labor relations in the public sector.

THE PUBLIC EMPLOYER

Belgium constitutes a constitutional hereditary monarchy, with a two-chamber parliament elected every four years: the Chamber of Representatives and a Senate.

The Chamber of Representatives consists of 212 members who are elected for four years unless the Chamber (and the Senate) is dissolved before that time has elapsed. Members must be at least 25 years of age, and they are elected by secret ballot according to the system of proportional representation. Suffrage is universal for citizens of twenty-one years or over.

The Senate, a second Chamber, is chosen in the following manner. It is composed of:

---

this trade union could—notwithstanding this nonparticipation—defend effectively the interests of its members in conformity with the ILO conventions regarding that matter.

1. Half as many members as the Chamber of Representatives, elected directly by the same electors.

2. Members chosen by the Provincial Councillors, in the proportion of one for every 200,000 population.

3. Members co-opted by groups 1 and 2, up to half the number of group 2. There are now 178 senators. All senators must be over age 40, with the exception of a small number of members of the Royal Family, who become senators by right at the age of 18.

Election is by party lists with a proportionately transferable vote, the effect of which is that big electoral swings are rare and governments are most frequently formed by coalition.

The King's place in the Belgian Constitution is very similar to the position of the Crown in Great Britain. Though he is, according to the terms of the Constitution, supreme head of the Executive, he in fact exercises his control through the Cabinet, which is responsible for all acts of the government to the legislative chambers. Though the King, according to the Constitution, appoints his own ministers, in practice, since they are responsible to the legislature, the Cabinet must enjoy the confidence of both chambers. Most Cabinet members are Members of Parliament.

Legislation is introduced either by the Government or the Members in the Houses, and as the party complexion of both Houses is generally almost the same, measures passed by the Chamber of Representatives are usually passed by the Senate and vice versa.

The actual Cabinet is a coalition of the Christian Social and Belgian Socialist parties, formed in June 1968. There are, besides the Prime Minister, 23 major Cabinet officers and two Minister-Secretaries of State. Most ministers have their own department (Foreign Affairs, National Defense, Agriculture, Public Works, National Education, Interior, Communications, Social Security, Justice, Labor, Health, Finance, Housing, Middle Class (self-employed small business people). An extensive number of decentralized agencies has been established. Some are directly governed by the competent ministers (for example, telegraph and telephone workers); the majority are more autonomous and operate under control of the competent minister, through the intervention of a government commissioner who can appeal against decisions which he thinks are contrary to the law, the statutes of the service, or the bonum commune. The Minister decides on this appeal. In all cases budgets are subject to cabinet's control and are approved by the Parliament or communicated to Parliament. For most of the decentralized agencies the status of personnel is determined by the Executive. Notable exceptions are Sabena and railroads, described below.

Belgium is divided into nine provinces (Antwerp, Brabant, East and West Flanders, Hainaut, Luxembourg, Liége, Namur, and Limburg). Although the provinces enjoy a certain degree of autonomy, the provincial structure is not federal.[5] The system of government of the provinces conforms to the general European practice based on a combination of central officials as the executive agent and locally elected councillers as the deliberating body. Each province has a Governor by Royal Appointment, and an elected Provincial Council, but their powers are limited to matters within their area and the National Parliament has unfettered competence in all matters of general policy, including finance. There are, of course, local taxation powers for local purposes, but a large part of these taxes is collected through the national fiscal machinery. The same goes for the local administrative unities, which are the municipalities. There are 2,590 municipalities, each of which has its Town Hall, its burgomaster and its elected City Council.

Trade Union Influence within Public Administration

Trade unions are omnipresent in the Belgian scenery. In numerous public services, trade union leaders are serving on

5. Under the Constitution the local and provincial authorities have a general competence for all problems of local and provincial importance. This general competence, somewhat vague, is exercised under control of the central authority, which can declare void local or provincial decisions if they are considered to be contrary to the general public interest. Appeal of any such decision lies with the Council of State (administrative court). The taxing authority of local provincial authorities is limited principally to the imposition of a tax on realty.

the board of governors or otherwise take part in the decision making.[6] As such, trade unions are not only influencing the outlook of the Belgian community through their numerous representatives in Parliament, in the provincial and the municipal councils, but also through the numerous administrative functions they perform. Unions are consulted on almost all matters regarding public life and certainly if any major changes affecting government employees are considered. In practice it is impossible for the Government to make any major decision without prior consultation, and often consent of the trade unions. It may already be indicated that following the Royal Decree of 1955 the trade union advisory councils are to be consulted for all matters involving the statutes of personnel, the organizations of the services, and safety of the establishment, as will be discussed in greater detail in the following chapter.

6. National Employment and Manpower Service; National Service for Family Allowances; National Service for Sickness and Invalidity Insurance; National Service for Blue-Collar Workers Pensions; National Fund for Work Accidents; National Fund for Professional Diseases; National Fund for Reclassification of Disabled People; National Fund for Annual Vacation; National Institute for Statistics; Committee for the Price-Index; Belgian Service for Increase of Productivity; Price Commission; National Committee for Economic Expansion; National Investment Corporation; Belgian Service for Foreign Commerce; National Society of Belgian Railroads; High Council for Social Tourism; National Bank; National Corporation for Credit Allowance to Industry; National Committee for Urbanization; High Council for the Family.

·IV·

Institutionalized Trade Union and Public Management Relations

THE TRADITIONAL PATTERN: ADVISORY COMMITTEES

THE aforementioned Royal Decree of 1955 provides for the creation of three different kinds of organs in which the trade unions are represented. These councils are bipartite.

At the top, a General Trade Union Council for Advice is established at the level of the Prime Minister. This council is headed by a president, appointed by the Prime Minister and further composed of 24 members. Twelve of those members are appointed by the trade unions, corresponding to the result of elections, which have to be held every four years. The other twelve are appointed by the Prime Minister. In order to be appointed, the latter public employees have at least to be "director of administration."[1]

A Trade Union Council for Advice is created in each department or public service, covered by the Royal Decree of 1955, where at least 100 employees are active. These councils are also headed by a president, appointed by the competent cabinet officer or the board of governors. There are minimum eight and maximum twenty members, according to the degree of employment within the department or service. Half of those members are appointed by the Minister or the Board of Governors, the other half by the trade unions, corresponding to the result of elections held every fourth year.

Personnel committees must be established per service or group of services, which employ at least 25 employees. They are composed along the same lines as developed under point 2 for the Trade Union Council for advice.

---

1. The Director of Administration is fifth in rank on the list of high level public servants, i.e., Secretary-General; Director-General; Inspector-General; Divisional Director; Director of Administration.

The function of the council and committees is to give advice on propositions about the statutes of personnel, the organization of the services, and of the work to be performed and safety, health and embellishment of the establishment. The advice of the general council has to be requested when the propositions affect employees occupied in different departments or services; the competent council's advice concerning propositions affecting the employees of one department or service and the competent personnel committee's advice when the propositions concern only that department or service. The personnel committees also perform the function of the safety and health committee. Advice is according to the majority of votes, and must be motivated by and give reference to the position of the minority. In case of equality of votes, the advice will mention both opinions. The president does not take part in the voting. Decisions made by the authorities must refer formally to the advice, and if they deviate from it, the reasons leading thereto must be communicated to the council or to the committee.

Trade unions are no longer contented with the advisory framework in which they have, legally at least, to operate. First of all, the advisory organs have no right to initiative: trade unions enjoy, within the advisory councils, only the right to give advice on propositions, unilaterally worked out by the competent authority. Their counterpart in the council, the representatives of the cabinet officers, have no real competence to decide on the matter discussed, and even unanimously agreed upon advices are not at all binding upon the competent authorities. Trade unions want to leave the advisory field and engage in bargaining with the competent authorities, this is to say, with those competent to make the appropriate and final decisions. This is what has already occurred in practice. In the previously mentioned national agreement of July 29, 1969, points b and c covered these items: "parties agreed that the new labor relations in the public sector should shift from consultation to negotiation. It was indicated that this (top) bargaining should be restricted to wages and other general labor conditions. Bargaining should take place following a well-detailed procedure in an ad hoc organ."

As indicated before, elections have to be held in principle every four years. The public employees vote for a particular trade union, not for individual candidates. The latest elections were held in 1959. Since then consequent elections have not been held, mainly at the request of the Christian and Socialist trade unions, who argue that elections within the actual chaotic system, with easy access to recognition, are nonsensical. As was already pointed out, the government has accepted organized trade union activity in the public sector on the basis of reserving collective bargaining for the most representative trade unions, thus practically forbidding the right of other unions to operate within the public sector.

The seats obtained by the different trade unions in the 1967 elections were:

Trade Union Organizations	Seats
Federation of Christian Trade Unions	5
Independent Unions	1
Liberal Trade Union	1
Socialist Trade Union	5

Trade unions intervene actively in merit rating and promotion and disciplinary measures taken against public employees. In case of merit rating and discipline, the individual employee can, within the scope of application of the Royal Decree of 1955, bring his case before the competent Council of Appeal. There are different councils of appeal following the hierarchy of employers. They are established only at the national level.

In these councils, which have an advisory competence, half the members are appointed by trade unions that have a seat on the trade union council for advice,[2] and the other half by the competent cabinet officer. Each public employee can confide his defense to a legal council (avocat) or to a trade

2. Exception is made for the Council of Appeal for top-ranking public employees (secretary- and director-general, for example) for which there is no union representation in the council of appeal.

union representative. The competent minister is not obliged to follow the advice of the council of appeal, but must explain his decision in case of dissent from the advice of the Council.

For the highest functions (secretary-general, director-general, inspector-general, director of administration, and first advisor), the competent cabinet officer has great freedom to promote the employee he thinks fit for the job. Here politics and trade union intervention play an extremely important role. Promotion toward jobs at lower levels has to take into account objective criteria, such as merit rating, seniority, and examinations. There are fewer possibilities for maneuvering, although trade unions remain influential.

THE NEW PATTERN: BARGAINING COMMITTEES

As already indicated, collective bargaining is already legally established in some sectors of public employment. This is particularly true in those government controlled agencies whose activities are closely linked or comparable to private industry and commerce, such as railroads, airways, tramways, and buses. Mention should also be made of the teachers of private schools. In these sectors joint committees are set up which operate along the same lines as the joint committees of the private sector, which was discussed earlier.

Railroads

The previously mentioned Act of July 23, 1926, creating the National Corporation of Belgian Railroads foresees in its Article 13 the establishment of a national joint committee, composed of 10 representatives of management and 10 representatives of the most representative trade unions.

The national joint committee is competent to: "Examine all questions regarding the individual labor contract, work accidents, accidents on the road to and from the work place, professional diseases, security hygiene, and all other questions regarding the interests of the personnel, give advice on all questions of a general nature which may be of indirect importance to the personnel; codetermine the social works, established to the benefit of the personnel."

The joint committee makes decisions with a majority of two thirds of the votes. Article 13 of the 1926 Act also permits the establishment of regional joint committees competent to examine suggestions by the employee concerning hygiene and security as well as regarding productivity. If no satisfaction can be obtained, those suggestions are referred to the board of governors, which can decide on those matters. The regional committees are also competent to give advice concerning the working regulation.

Airways—Sabena

The national joint committee, competent for air transport, was created by Royal Decree of March 24, 1961. This joint committee operates following the same lines as the joint committees in the private sector. It should be noted also that a union delegation and working council are set up within Sabena. This leads us to conclude that labor relations in Sabena are quite identical with those of the private sector.

Teachers in Private Schools

The Act of May 29, 1959, concerning the private schools (primary, high, technical, and teacher training schools) provides for the creation of joint committees. Joint committees, composed of an equal number of the representative organizations of schools and of trade unions, were set up as follows: a general joint committee, competent for matters dealing with the four school branches and four specific joint committees respectively for primary, high, technical, and teacher training schools. (This differentiation of competence between the general and the specific committees is not at all clear. In fact, the general committee actually does not function.) Following the act, joint committees are competent to deliberate on general labor conditions and have the functions of preventing conflicts. Decisions are taken with unanimous vote and are only binding if they are rendered obligatory by Royal Decree.

The main observation which must be made is undoubtedly

that the law and other government regulations take care of almost all working and labor conditions of the teachers (wages, hours, social security, pensions, etc.). This is done within the framework of government subsidies to the private school system; these subventions among other things cover 100 percent of the wages of teachers in private schools. Practically, the joint committees have competence in the field of job security and discipline, but as stated, their decisions are only binding if approved by Royal Decree. This means that the main point of decision-making is to influence the national government, which decides upon wages and working conditions of all teachers, within public or private schools, in a centralized manner.

PROVINCES AND MUNICIPALITIES[3]

Labor relations on the level of provinces and municipalities are not regulated, either by government regimentation or by collective agreement. At one time an advisory body was set up at the level of the Department of the Interior in which the Christian, Socialist, and Liberal trade unions were represented. This body does not function any longer. To find out how wages and working conditions, especially in municipalities, are regulated is an almost impossible assignment.

3. This includes health personnel, public hospitals, public safety employees and policemen. It should, however, be pointed out that trade union representatives, or trade union backed politicians, are heavily represented in the municipal and provincial councils, as well as in the college of burgomaster and aldermen and the permanent deputation.

· V ·

Collective Bargaining in the Public Sector

OUR analysis up to now shows clearly that actually two types of trade union management relations can be discerned in the public sector: one model is the traditional type of consultation, where trade unions are molded in advisory machinery, leading to a government decision; the other model is one of collective bargaining, already existent in some government controlled industries and the "social programmation agreements," covering the whole public sector already referred to. This bargaining is heavily influenced by the cabinet system and the centralized setting of wages and working conditions in the public sector.

THE CABINET SYSTEM

Concentrating on the organization and authority for bargaining on the employer's side, labor relations and the setting of wages and working conditions are marked by two characteristics of the utmost importance. Both have already been mentioned: (1) the Cabinet system and (2) centralization, which operates within the Belgian administrative system.

The Cabinet system functions as well on the national, provincial, and local level. This is to say that the Executive has to have the confidence of an elected council. These are the relations between the National Cabinet and the Parliament, the permanent deputation (headed by the governor) and the provincial council and the college of mayor and aldermen and the municipality council. The different executives (national government, permanent deputation and college of burgomaster and aldermen) are the microcosm of and responsible to their respective legislatures. Thus, the budgetary measures and other legislative actions, necessary to implement the decisions or agreements made by the Executives are almost automatically taken by the legislatures.

The principal difficulty, however, is to arrive at a decision, as the decision-making power is so scattered around, and so many offices, administrations, and departments are involved, before a decision can be reached at the different relevant levels. By and large, one can say that the actual administrative set-up is not intended for bargaining purposes. Trade unions rightly complain that they too often have to deal with individuals who have no authority to decide. However, ways and means are found to remedy this situation, as is clearly shown by the "social programmation" in which bargaining takes place with the Prime Minister and some of the high-ranking Cabinet officials themselves. No wonder that the national agreement of January 26, 1968, promises that bargaining will be structured following detailed procedures and in an organization created for that purpose.

CENTRALIZATION OF DECISION MAKING

The power to decide upon wages and working conditions of public employees belongs in principle to the authority who has the competence to appoint the public employee. The status of national civil servants as such is regulated by the national government (the Executive), while municipal workers' conditions are laid down by the council of the municipality. The same goes for provincial workers and the like.

However, there is a more or less national governmental centralized setting of wages and working conditions due to numerous practical reasons. The most important is the fact that the so-called autonomous municipalities, provinces, and decentralized agencies need to have their decisions in one way or another approved by the central government, and are for their financial resources largely dependent on national government subventions. Theoretically, the municipalities have the competence to set the wages and working conditions of their employees, although in practice they get instructions from the Department of the Interior, which, if followed up by the right decisions, will get the necessary department approval. In cases where wages and working conditions (for example, for magistrates, army, and national guard) are, following constitutional requirements, to be regulated by the national Parliament, the competent departments in fact make the decisions, which, due to the Cabinet system, will be approved by Parliament.

As such, although theoretically speaking, the decisions belong to the national Parliament itself, the provincial council, the municipal council or the board of a decentralized agency, the main patterns of wages and working conditions are set by the national administration. This is the department of authority, in close connection with the Department for the Public Office (Fonction Publique). Above all, in many cases the law has intervened to set rules on pensions: laws which are prepared by the Government and adopted by Parliament.

In other words, the main locus of decision-making is the national government; consequently trade unions focus their attention mainly on the national administration as far as general wages and working conditions are concerned. One example: teachers employed in the municipal schools are appointed by the municipal council, which is also theoretically competent to fix their wages and working conditions. However, municipal schools are subsidized by the national government, in particular the wages of teachers. These subventions go along with a detailed set of regulations, concerning the number of teachers to be subventioned (corresponding to the number of children present at school), the administrative hierarchy within the school, and the like. In other words, the formal decisions belong to the municipality. The real decisions covering wages and working conditions are general and nationwide, made by the Department for Education and Culture in close connection with the Minister for Public Office and other departments (like Finance and Budget), as the budget, providing the subventions, has to be approved by Parliament.

THE SOCIAL PROGRAMMATION AGREEMENTS

Social programmation in the public sector developed fully in the beginning of this decade.[1] Programmation means basically

1. This social programmation between trade unions and employers was enacted in the private sector by the Pact of Social Programmation of May 11, 1960, which covers the private sector as a whole and laid down three fundamental principles: (1) A concerted policy of economic

that social progress, taking into account economic possibilities, is jointly planned by employers and trade unions on a national level. Since 1962, national agreements, covering the public sector as a whole, were consecutively concluded. A first agreement (July 1, 1962) covered the period July 1, 1962, to December 31, 1964. The second agreement (January 1, 1965) was a one-year agreement, while the third (December 22, 1965) covered the years 1966-67. The fourth agreement (January 26, 1968) was equally spread over two years, 1968-69. The last and fifth agreement, July 29, 1969, covers the years 1970-71.

The agreements cover in principle all public employees, namely, of the national departments,[2] the decentralized agencies, provinces, municipalities, teachers (as well of the private sector). It is amazing that it covers also the pensioned employees as their pension allowances are improved.

Social programmation is, as such, centralized to a great extent. Besides covering all public employees, it is conducted by the two big unions representing all public employees at one side, and the national government on the other side. Both unions act as "a common front." This means that they meet in order to fix common goals and claims, which will be submitted to government. As such, the government bargains in fact with one partner,[3] which of course considerably facilitates bargaining.

Until 1968 the agreements were written "protocols" (memoranda) not signed by the partners. Since the agreement of January 26, 1968, they are called "collective agreements," not only in the sense of the result of bargaining, but also formally signed by partners. The latest agreement is signed by the representatives

---

expansion must enable workers to share in a regularly improving standard of living. (2) This participation of the workers in the improvement of their standard of living must be realized through collective agreements, concluded at national interindustry level, by which the share of workers in the growth of the national wealth is programmed for a fixed period. National agreements by industry sector and agreements at the plant level must program supplementary advantages. The programmation will, however, take into account governmental social security benefits, financed through employer contributions. (3) This programmation is possible only if industrial peace is observed during the life of the collective agreements.

2. Even the army and national guard.

3. This "common front" exists also in the private sector.

of the two trade unions at one side, the Prime Minister, the Vice-Premier and the Minister of the Public Function at the other side.

Bargaining has in principle to take into account the tax year, as the financial implications have to be taken care of in the corresponding yearly budgets. However this does not necessarily mean that bargaining takes place on fixed dates or per year. Until now, the national collective agreements in the public sector covered mostly a period of two years. The new benefits are, however, mostly spread over the two years, each year separately taken. Until recently, the agreements did not precede the budget-making process. The latest agreement, however, was negotiated and concluded far in advance, preceding the budget-making process. The procedure which has been developed, along practical lines, goes as follows and may be illustrated by the completion of the latest agreement of 1969.

On March 10, 1969, both trade unions (Christian and Socialist) presented their joint program of demands to the Prime Minister. In agreement with the Minister for the Public Function and the two unions, a working party was set up to examine the financial costs of the different demands of the unions. This working party was presided over by the Chief of Cabinet of the Minister of Public Function, seven trade union representatives and ten high-ranking public servants.[4]

This working group estimated the costs of the different claims and deposed its report on June 1, 1969. Since that time, regular meetings between the Premier and his colleagues of Budget, Labor, Public Function and Transport on one side, and the Common Front on the other side, took place. This ultimately led to the conclusion of the agreement of July 29, 1969. As the agreement covers the period of January 1, 1970, to December 31, 1971, there is ample time to adopt the budget and enact new regulations to implement the agreement.

Different considerations have to be made here. Although the actual timing of the agreement corresponds to the normal desire of having bargaining precede or coincide with the budget-making

4. Departments of Interior, Public Function, Finance, and Budget were represented at this working party.

process, it is done so that if bargaining takes place at a later date, Parliament can still adjust the budget afterwards, which happens to be a normal practice in the Belgian parliamentary system.

Secondly, it must be pointed out that wages and benefits in Belgium, in the private as well as in the public sector, are linked to the cost of living as a matter of government policy, so that the exact volume of wages is always up to that point uncertain. Not much is known about what actually happens at the bargaining table between the government and trade unions. It appears, however, that the government, taking into account its own overall budget, has proposed a certain maximum amount that could be distributed. Comparing the agreement at one side and the original union claims at the other side it appears that the government did really bargain and not giveway.

Social programmation bargaining for all employees included many issues, varying from agreement to agreement. The agreement for December 22, 1966, covered fixing minimum wages, special allowances, and additional vacation pay; it also dealt with the restructuring of railroad employment, education, pensions, industrial accidents, a cost-of-living clause, trade union relations in the public sector, and other issues. The agreements of January 26, 1968, and July 29, 1969, covered similar issues. In essence, the different points of agreements are not only broad in scope but rather simple in expression, as, for example, a 3 percent wage increase for all employees.[5]

5. The translated text of the fifth national programmation agreement of July 29, 1969, can be found in Appendix I. It must be taken into account that there is a Belgian tradition of regulating a number of working conditions through legislation; this is also true for the private sector. Also in making this legislation, trade unions through direct intervention at the level of Cabinet officers or through their political representatives in Parliament are actively involved and quite successful in obtaining results. Many questions that are the subject of collective bargaining in the USA or in Great Britain are governed by law in Belgium. Acts concerning individual contracts for blue-collar workers regulate, among other things, the different forms of contracts, damages of breach thereof, layoff, period of notice prior to dismissal, illness, working time, overtime, female and child labor, safety and working conditions, holidays with pay, paid annual leaves and the like. There is also very detailed social security regulations dealing with unemployment, sickness and health insurance, pensions, occupational diseases and family allowances.

These agreements are as such not enforceable. They only bring into plan the political responsibility of the national government to take the necessary legislative, executive, and other steps to implement the agreements. The agreement of July 29, 1969, foresees that the national government will take the necessary measures leading to the legislative and regulatory implications of the agreement itself and invite the decentralized agencies, provinces, and municipalities to make the formal decisions to implement the obligations contracted by the government. This means that the national government, as was already implied, is taking responsibilities it is technically not entitled to, which clearly illustrates the centralized setting of wages and labor conditions in the public sector.

It should be added that the trade unions, on the occasion of the conclusion of the agreement of 1969, expressly stated that if changes in the economic, financial, or monetary situation of the country occurred affecting the employees' purchasing power, the unions would consider themselves free to start pushing for adjustments. Things are even more complicated. Earlier, we indicated that the advisory councils, set up following the Royal Decree of 1955, have an advisory function on the status of personnel, the organization of the services and safety and health. This means first of all that for formal reasons the content of the national "social programmation" agreement has still to go through the advisory machinery, even after the agreement has been negotiated, which is, of course, a mere formality.

SECTORIAL AGREEMENTS

The over-all national agreement leaves room for additional bargaining or consultation in the different sectors. The latest national agreement of July 29, 1969, provides rather vaguely that "measures per sector, category, as well as regional or local measures can be taken within certain limits to be agreed upon." This means that the national programmation is in fact a first step, on top of which further bargaining can be undertaken, where this is possible—for railroads and Sabena or that another point can be decided upon at lower levels.

Detailed provisions are found in the sectorial agreements,

as for example railroads. The different decisions taken by the joint committee fill quite a book. They concern recruitment, wages and fringe benefits, promotion, working time, duties of personnel, vacation, social works, sickness, vocational training and retraining, trade union activity, disciplinary rules, termination of employment, pensions, invalidity and the like.

·VI·

Strikes and the Settlement of Disputes

IN Belgium, strikes in the public sector were condemned until recently by unanimous legal doctrine, although not by specific legislation. Among the traditional arguments used to deny public employees the freedom to strike, the "law of continuity" was prevalent. The idea was that public services were established only because they are considered to be indispensable to society and may as such not be prevented from functioning. Many authors actually reason that strikes are not expressly forbidden and as such are not unlawful, excepting the army and national guard. Moreover, trade unions, in getting their recognition under the decree of June 1955, had to submit their bylaws to the competent Cabinet officer. Now, the bylaws of most trade unions contain articles claiming the right to strike. It is only the Department of Defense which has informed trade unions that it could not accept its workers (mainly on military bases) striking. The other departments have recognized the trade unions, without raising any objections as to the provisions of the union's bylaws relative to the use of the right to strike.

Whatever the legal point of view may be, strikes are called for, although they are rather rare. Trade unions are convinced that immoderate use of strikes may lead to their ineffectiveness. Consequently, they look upon strikes only as an ultimate solution. It should be noted that both the CSC and the FGTB have substantial strike funds at their disposal. In principle there can be sanctions in the case of strikes; in practice, except for rare occasions, no sanctions are taken. Even the salaries of strikers are not withheld.

The fact that it was for a long time accepted that strikes and public service are "contradictio interminis" combined with the formalistic outlook and shape of wages and working conditions through unilateral government regulation has meant that there are no rules on strikes, neither on settlement of disputes and in principle no rules concerning the requirement of certain services, as these exist in the private sector. The Act of August 19, 1948, dealing with essential supplies and services in peace time, stipulates a procedure by which public interest and equipment are protected in case of a strike. It is, however, up to the joint committees to decide what supplies and services have to be maintained. Their decisions are put into operation by a subcommittee designated by the joint committee. If no decision or proper action is taken by the joint committee, the government can intervene and requisition workers. Although this law applies in principle only to the private sector it also covers gas, electricity, ports, urban tramways, and buses, which are part of public services. Other laws provide for requisitioning of persons, which in principle also apply to the public sector, but their stipulations are very vague and broad in nature and they are only rarely applied. The government, as a political power, is rather reluctant to intervene and has to reckon upon the sense of responsibility trade unions have.

If strikes occur, they are currently settled on the basis of accepting improved conditions. Public employee unions place their main emphasis on economic objectives, that is, wages and working conditions. Strikes, if they happen, are only rarely political in nature, as for example the general strike of 1960-61 (December-January) against the government. Strikes in the Department of Finance (1963), of policemen (Antwerp-1967), postal workers (Brussels-1969), and in radio-television (1969) were only concerned with the status of employees.

One example: television and radio personnel organized a strike (July 8-17, 1969). The board of governors of radio and television had appointed a personnel manager, who did not come out of the ranks of the television or radio personnel. The board was legally entitled to make the appointment but was forced, under pressure of the strike, to cancel it. On this occasion the trade unions raised objections, namely concerning the organization of the radio and television personnel (unions asked the abolishment of the actual board of governors, who are mainly political appointees), codetermination, improved wages, promotions and real collective bargaining, which were referred for further discussion.

Arbitration of industrial disputes, whether of basic agreements or grievances, is almost unknown in Belgium. The trade unions, the CSC and the FGTB reject both compulsory and voluntary arbitration because in their view the freedom to strike would thereby become meaningless. Neither is any machinery for conciliation, as it exists in the private sector, established. Problems and disputes are regulated through continuous contact between the trade unions.

This contact exists also between parties in order to interpret national agreements. The most recent agreement of social programmation of July 29, 1969, allows the establishment of a joint committee, under the presidency of the minister of public function to supervise the implementation and the application of the agreement, as well as its interpretation. As such, it is up to the parties themselves to interpret their own agreement and to settle their own "disputes of rights." (It must, however, be repeated that this collective agreement is implemented through laws and decrees. As far as their interpretation in individual cases is concerned, the normal courts are competent.) This is typical for Belgian labor relations. The social partners want to settle differences without intervention of third parties.

CONCLUSIONS

Public employee unionism in Belgium is undoubtedly molded by the political and administrative system of Belgian government. Labor relations and the setting of wages and working conditions are marked by two characteristics of the utmost importance: the cabinet system on one side and the centralized setting of wages and working conditions on the other. The cabinet system implies that the executive, which negotiates, will find the legislature almost automatically willing to implement the decisions or agreements by the necessary budgetary measures and other legislative action.

The centralization of wages and working conditions has

as a consequence that the national government is the main locus of decision-making, meaning that trade unions concentrate their efforts at the level of the national administration. It cannot be stressed enough that these trade unions, at least the most representative, have far-reaching influence in the public sector, given their close links with the major political parties, and the part they take in the decision-making in a great number of public services.

Drastic changes are occurring in the character and nature of trade union-management relations in the public sector. The Royal Decree of 1955 is still the only legal basis entitling trade union action for an important part of the public sector. This Royal Decree sets conditions for trade union recognition and allows an advisory role for the trade unions. The most representative trade unions, namely the Christian and the Socialist trade unions, complain bitterly about the ease with which recognition especially specific recognition, can be obtained. Practically speaking, the most representative trade unions want to establish for themselves a monopoly of trade union action in the public sector of the same format as that in the private sector. The national government has accepted this point of view and has agreed to take the necessary measures toward that end.

The advisory function of trade unions, foreseen by the Royal Decree, is as such bound to disappear. It still goes on now, but in the shadow of collective bargaining, which is the general practice.

Except for a few decentralized agencies, whose activities are closely linked or comparable to private industry and commerce, as railroads, airways and the like, collective bargaining in the public sector is relatively new. Social programmation bargaining in the public sector developed fully with the beginning of the 1960's. The national collective agreements, covering mostly a period of two years, are a typical example of centralized bargaining. Beside covering all public employees, they are negotiated by the two big trade unions on one side, and the national government on the other side. In fact the government bargains with one partner as both unions act as a "common front." These agreements are formally signed by the Prime Minister and other cabinet officers as well as by the representatives of the trade unions. The latest agreement, covering the years 1970-71, was signed on July 29, 1969, preceding the budget making process. This collective bargaining, which covers a whole range of wages and working conditions, is not at all regulated. Devices such as notifications, timetables, mediation or publicized neutral recommendations, are unknown. Collective bargaining relies on practices and continuous contact between the social partners. It would be difficult to ascertain that bargaining takes place over shares of fixed sums, or is affected by a real "incomes policy," which is nonexistent in Belgium. The social programmation agreements are not enforceable. They only engage the political responsibility for the national governments to take the necessary legislative, executive, and other steps to implement the agreements.

In the various departments and other public services informal bargaining, not all structured, is conducted more or less on a day-to-day basis. It is beyond doubt that these will become more and more formalized under the umbrella of the overall social programmation.

Appendix I

Act of Freedom of Association

ACT TO REPEAL SECTION 310 OF THE PENAL CODE

Sole Section. Section 310[1] of the Penal Code, as amended by the Act of 30 May 1892, is hereby repealed.

24 May 1921

ACT TO GUARANTEE FREEDOM OF ASSOCIATION

1. Universal freedom of association is hereby guaranteed. No person shall be compelled to join or refrain from joining any association.

2. Any person who applies for membership in an association shall undertake, by the fact of becoming a member, to submit to the rules of the association in question and to the decisions and penalties adopted under the said rules. He may withdraw from the association, in conformity with the rules, at any time; any provision in the rules which denies his liberty to do so shall be void.

3. Any person who, for the purpose of compelling a particular individual to join or refrain from joining an association, resorts

1. Section 310. The penalties of imprisonment for one month to two years and a fine of 50 to 100 francs, or one of these penalties, shall be imposed on any person who, with the object of exacting an increase or decrease of wages or interfering with the free exercise of industry or labour, commits violence, makes use of insults or threats, the imposition of fines, prohibitions, interdicts or proscriptions of any kind whatever, against those who work themselves or cause work to be done.

The same provision shall apply to all who interfere with the freedom of masters or workers, whether by assembling near the establishments in which work is being carried on or near the dwellings of the persons directing the work, or by acts of intimidation directed against workers on their way to or from work, or by causing explosions near the establishments in which work is being carried on or in districts inhabited by workers, or by breaking down the fences of the establishments in which work is being carried on or of the dwellings or land occupied by the workers, or by destroying or rendering unfit for their proper use the tools, instruments, appliances, and apparatus of work or industry.

to violence, molestation or threats, or who causes him to fear the loss of his employment or injury to his person, family or property, shall be punished by imprisonment from one week to one month and a fine of 50 to 500 francs, or by one of these penalties.

4. Any person who, with intent to attack freedom of association, makes the conclusion, the execution or (even with due regard to customary notice) the continuance of a contract of work or service conditional upon the affiliation or nonaffiliation of one or more persons to an association, shall be liable to the same penalties.

5. By way of exception from Section 100 of the Penal Code, Chapter 7 and Section 85 of Book I of the said Code shall apply to the contraventions mentioned in this Act.[2]

24 May 1921

2. Chapter VII of the Penal Code defines persons who are to be deemed partners or accomplices in a crime or offence. Section 85 specifies the extent to which penalties can be reduced on account of extenuating circumstances.

Appendix II

Act Respecting Collective Industrial Agreements and Joint Committees

CHAPTER I. INTRODUCTORY PROVISIONS

1.

In this Act:

(1) "the agreement" shall mean a collective industrial agreement;

(2) "the Minister" shall mean the Minister responsible for labour affairs;

(3) "the joint body" shall mean the National Labour Council, the joint committees and the joint subcommittees;

(4) "the organization" shall mean the employers' representative organizations and the workers' representative organizations referred to in section 3.

2.

1. This Act shall apply to workers and employers and to their organizations.

For the purpose of this Act, the following shall be considered as:

(1) a worker: a person who, other than by virtue of a contract of employment,[1] performs work under the authority of another person;

(2) an employer: a person who gives work to a person fulfilling clause;

(3) a contract of employment: the employment relationship between persons deemed to be workers and employers;

1. The term "contrat de travail" (contract of service) is that employed in Belgian legislation for workmen's contracts of service, other expressions such as "contract de louage de travail" (contract of employment) being used for the contracts of service of domestic servants, homeworkers, apprentices, seamen and salaried employees. The term "contrat d'emploi" is that used in relation to "employés" and is translated as "contract of salaried employment."

(4) a branch of activity: groups of persons considered as employers who, outside a sector of the economy, carry on identical or related activities;

(5) an undertaking: the establishment of a person considered as an employer.

Source: Moniteur Belge, 15 January 1969, No. 10, p. 267.

2. The fact that the contract of employment is null and void shall not constitute grounds for nonapplication of this Act, where the work is performed:

(1) under a contract of employment declared null and void on the grounds of violation of the legislation regulating the employment relationship;

(2) in gaming establishments.

3. This Act shall not apply to:

(1) persons employed by the State, the provinces, the communes, public establishments owned or operated by the above and quasi-public or officially recognized bodies:

Provided that the Crown may, by order stating the grounds on which it is based and discussed and adopted by the Council of Ministers, extend in full or in part the application of this Act to the above-mentioned persons or certain categories of them;

(2) persons employed in sheltered workshops or in vocational training centers under the legislation respecting the resettlement of handicapped persons[2] or the legislation respecting employment and unemployment.[3]

3.

For the purposes of the application of this Act, the following shall be deemed to be workers' representative organizations and employers' representative organizations:

(1) interoccupational organizations of workers and employers established at the national level and represented on the Central Economic Council and the National Labour Council; the workers' organization shall furthermore have at least 50,000 members;

2. Cf. *Legislative Series,* 1963—Bel. 1.
3. Ibid., 1963—Bel. 2., 1967—Bel. 2 A.

(2) the occupational organizations affiliated to, or forming part of, an interoccupational organization referred to in paragraph (1);

(3) the employers' occupational organizations which, in any given branch of activity, are declared to be representative by the Crown on the advice of the National Labour Council.

The national interoccupational and occupational organizations approved under the Act of 6 March 1964 to provide for the institutional structure of the middle classes which are representative of heads of undertakings in handicrafts, small and medium trades and small-scale industry and self-employed persons carrying on a liberal profession or other professional type of work shall also be deemed to be representative employers' organizations.

4.

The organizations shall have the capacity to sue and be sued in all litigation arising out of the application of this Act, and to defend their members' rights arising out of the agreements concluded by them. This representation by the organizations shall not affect the right of the members to bring an action individually on their own behalf, to join in the action or to intervene therein at any stage: Provided that damages for nonperformance of the obligations arising out of an agreement may be claimed from organizations only in so far as the agreement expressly provides for this.

Unless their rules contain a stipulation to the contrary, the organizations shall be represented in legal proceedings by the person responsible for the day-to-day management.

CHAPTER II. COLLECTIVE LABOUR AGREEMENTS

Division 1. Definition and Contents

5.

The term "collective industrial agreement" means an agreement concluded between one or more workers' organizations and one or more employers' organizations or one or more employers, stipulating the individual and collective relations between employers and workers in undertakings or in a branch of activity, and regulating the rights and obligations of the contracting parties.

6.

The agreement may be made, within a joint body, by one or more workers' organizations and one or more employers' organizations and, outside a joint body, by one or more workers' organizations and one or more employers' organizations or one or more employers.

7.

The scope of an agreement concluded in the National Labour Council shall cover different branches of activity throughout the entire country: Provided that an agreement may be concluded in the National Labour Council for a branch of activity which is not within the competence of an establishment joint committee or where an established joint committee does not function.

8.

The Crown shall decide, on a recommendation to this effect from the joint committee, whether the agreements concluded in a joint subcommittee referred to in section 37 require the endorsement of the joint committee. If endorsement is required, the joint committee shall make its decision within the month following the date on which the agreement is transmitted to it, failing which the agreement shall be deemed to be endorsed.

9.

The provisions of an agreement which

(1) are contrary to the peremptory provisions of Acts and other statutory instruments, treaties and international agreements which have binding force in Belgium;

(2) provide for the settlement of individual disputes by arbitrators shall be null and void.

10.

The following shall be null and void:

(1) the provisions of an agreement concluded in a joint committee which are contrary to an agreement concluded in the National Labour Council;

(2) the provisions of an agreement concluded in a joint sub-committee which are contrary to an agreement concluded in the National Labour Council or in the joint committee of which it is a subcommittee;

(3) the provisions of an agreement concluded outside a joint body which are contrary to an agreement concluded in the National Labour Council or a joint committee or joint subcommittee which is competent for the undertakings concerned.

11.

The clauses of a contract of employment and the provisions of work rules which are contrary to those of a collective industrial agreement binding the employers and workers concerned shall be null and void.

Division 2. Conclusion and Termination

12.

The delegates of the organizations shall be presumed to have the power to conclude the agreement on behalf of their organization. This presumption shall be irrefutable.

If the agreement is concluded in the National Labour Council, all the organizations referred to in section 3, clause (2), shall be deemed to be one sole organization represented by the members nominated on the recommendation of the High Council for the Middle Classes.

13.

Any agreement not made in writing shall be null and void.

The agreement shall be drafted in French and Dutch:

Provided that it shall be drafted only in the language of the region concerned if it refers exclusively to the French-language region, the Dutch-language region or the German-language region.

14.

The agreement shall be signed by the persons concluding it on behalf of their organization or in their own name. These signatures may be replaced by

(1) a statement to the effect that the chairman and the

secretary of the joint body have signed the minutes of the meeting approved by the members;

(2) the signature of a member of each organization represented on the joint body in which the agreement was concluded;

(3) the signature of the person who brought about conciliation between the parties in the case of a labor dispute and who testifies that the parties have indicated their agreement on the written record of conciliation.

15.

The agreement concluded shall be of specified duration, of unspecified duration or of specified duration with a renewal clause.

Unless there is a stipulation to the contrary, an agreement of unspecified duration or an agreement of specified duration with a renewal clause may be terminated, with prior notice, by either of the parties. Notice of partial termination shall be permissible only if there is an express stipulation to this effect in the agreement.

Notice of intention to terminate which is not made in writing shall be null and void.

16.

It shall be compulsory to give the following information in each agreement:

(1) the name of the organizations concluding the agreement;

(2) the name of the joint body, if the agreement is concluded in such body;

(3) the identity of the persons concluding the agreement and, if the agreement is concluded outside a joint body, the capacity in which such persons act and, where applicable, their functions in their organization;

(4) the person, the branch of activity or the undertakings and the territory to which the agreement applies, unless the agreement is binding on all the employers and workers covered by the joint body in which it is concluded;

(5) the duration of validity of an agreement of specified duration, or the modes of termination and period of prior notice to terminate an agreement of unspecified duration or

an agreement of specified duration containing a renewal clause;

(6) the date of coming into force, if the agreement does not come into force on the date of its conclusion;

(7) the date on which the agreement was concluded;

(8) the signature of the persons having capacity to sign in accordance with the provisions of section 14, or the statement provided for in that section.

17.

Organizations and employers which were not parties to the conclusion of the agreement may subsequently accede thereto at any time, subject to the assent of all the parties to the agreement, unless the agreement contains provision to the contrary.

Accession which is not stipulated in writing shall be null and void.

18.

The agreement shall be deposited with the Ministry of Employment and Labour. Deposit shall not be accepted if the agreement fails to fulfil the conditions laid down in sections 13, 14, and 16.

The following documents shall be deposited at the Ministry of Employment and Labour:

(1) the accession of an organization or employer to the agreement;

(2) notice of intention to terminate an agreement of specified duration or an agreement of specified duration containing a renewal clause.

Any person may obtain a copy of the agreement deposited on payment of a fee, the amount of which shall be fixed by the Crown.

Division 3. Persons and Bodies Bound by the Agreement

19.

The agreement shall be binding on

(1) the organizations which concluded it and the employers who are members of such organizations which have considered the agreement, as from the date of its coming into force;

(2) the organizations and employers subsequently acceding to

the agreement, and the employers' members of such organizations, as from the date of their accession;

(3) employers who become affiliated to an organization bound by the agreement, as from the date of their affiliation;

(4) all the workers in the service of an employer bound by the agreement.

20.

In the case of the total or partial transfer of an undertaking, the new employer shall be bound to observe the terms of the agreement which bound the former employer, until the agreement is no longer in force.

21.

An employer whose affiliation to an organization bound by the agreement comes to an end shall remain bound by the said agreement unless and until the terms of the said agreement are so amended as to bring about a considerable modification of the obligations arising out of the agreement.

22.

In the case of the dissolution of an organization bound by an agreement, the rules governing the individual relations between employers and workers drawn up by virtue of the agreement shall continue to apply to the members of the organization until the agreement itself is so amended as to bring about a considerable modification of the said relations.

23.

An individual contract of employment modified implicitly by a collective agreement shall remain unchanged if the agreement ceases to be in force, unless there is a stipulation to the contrary in the agreement itself.

Division 4. Agreements Concluded in a Joint Body

24.

In a given joint body the agreement shall be concluded by all the organizations which are represented on that body.

25.

The object, date, duration, scope and place of deposit on an agreement concluded in a joint body shall be published by notice inserted in the *Moniteur Belge*. Notice of intention to terminate an agreement of unspecified duration or an agreement of specified duration containing a renewal clause shall also be published by notice inserted in the *Moniteur Belge*.

26.

The clauses of an agreement concluded in a joint body which deal with individual relations between employers and workers shall bind all employers and workers other than those referred to in section 19, who are covered by the joint body, in so far as they fall within the scope of the agreement, unless the individual contract of employment contains a written clause to the contrary. This provision shall apply as from the fifteenth day following the publication referred to in section 25, first paragraph.

27.

In the case of modification of the scope of a joint committee or joint subcommittee, the agreements concluded within the latter shall continue to be binding on the employers and workers to which they applied before such modification, until such time as the committee or subcommittee within whose jurisdiction they fall after such modifications as arranged for the application to be said employers and workers of agreements concluded in such committee or subcommittee.

Division 5. Declaration as to General Binding Force

28.

An agreement concluded in a joint body may be declared generally binding by the Crown at the request of the joint body or an organization represented on the same.

29.

If the Minister is of the opinion that he should not recommend to the Crown to make the agreement generally binding he shall make known the reasons of his decision to the joint body concerned.

30.

The operative part of the agreement rendered generally binding shall be published in the *Moniteur Belge,* annexed to the Royal Order declaring it to be generally binding.

Where the agreement is drafted in one language only, publication shall be made also in Dutch and French.

31.

An agreement rendered generally binding shall bind all the employers and workers falling within the jurisdiction of the joint body, in so far as they fall within the scope stipulated in the agreement.

32.

The Royal Order declaring an agreement to be generally binding shall come into force on the date of coming into force of the agreement itself: Provided that it may not have retroactive effect for more than one year preceding the date of its publication.

33.

The Royal Order declaring a collective agreement of specified duration to be generally binding shall cease to have effect on the expiration of the specified duration of the agreement. If notice of intention to terminate an agreement of unspecified duration or an agreement of specified duration containing a renewal clause has been properly served, the Order declaring the agreement to be generally binding shall be repealed by the Crown with effect from the date on which the agreement is terminated.

34.

The Crown may repeal the entire Order declaring an agreement to be generally binding, or part of such Order, if and to the extent that the agreement no longer meets with the situation or fulfils the conditions which justified the declaration making it generally binding:

Provided that the Minister may recommend to the Crown the repeal of the said Order only if the joint body in which the agreement was concluded gives its consent to such repeal.

The Crown may also repeal the Order declaring an agreement to be generally binding if the latter contains a provision which is null and void by virtue of sections 9 or 10. If the provision becomes null on a date later than the date on which the Order comes into force, the Order shall be repealed as from the later date. If the Minister is considering making a recommendation to the Crown to repeal an Order pursuant to the third paragraph of this section, he shall give prior notice to this effect to the body concerned.

CHAPTER III. JOINT COMMITTEES

Division 1. Establishment and Competence

35.

The Crown may, on its own initiative or on the request of one or more organizations, establish joint committees of employers and workers. It shall specify the persons, the branch of activity or the undertakings and the territorial scope of each committee.

36.

Whenever the Minister considers recommending to the Crown the establishment of a joint committee or the alteration of the scope of an existing committee, he shall so inform the organizations concerned by notice published in the *Moniteur Belge*.

37.

At the request of a joint committee the Crown may establish one or more joint subcommittees. After consulting the joint committee concerned, the Crown shall specify the persons and territory covered by the said subcommittees.

38.

The joint committees and subcommittees shall:

(1) collaborate in the drafting of collective industrial agreements by the organizations represented;

(2) prevent or bring about the conciliation of disputes between employers and workers;

(3) advise the Government, the National Labour Council, the

Central Economic Council or the trades councils on matters falling within their competence, at the latter's request or on the committee's or subcommittee's own initiative;

(4) carry out any other task imposed on them by law or by virtue of the law.

Where action is required to be taken by the joint committees by law or by virtue of any statutory provision, the National Labour Council shall take such action in cases where a joint committee has not been set up or where a joint committee set-up is not functioning.

Division 2. Composition

39.

The joint committees and subcommittees shall be composed of:

(1) a chairman and a vice-chairman;

(2) an equal number of representatives of employers' organizations and workers' organizations;

(3) two or more secretaries.

40.

The Crown shall nominate the chairman and vice-chairman from among persons competent in social affairs but not involved in the interests with which the joint committee or subcommittee may be concerned. The function of chairman and vice-chairman shall be incompatible with holding office as Member of one of the Houses of Parliament.

The vice-chairman shall replace the chairman whenever the latter is unable to act. If the vice-chairman is unable to act, he shall be replaced by a civil service officer designated by the Minister. In discharging their duties the chairman and vice-chairman shall be under the authority of the Minister.

41.

The Crown shall fix the number of members of each joint committee and subcommittee; there shall be as many substitute members as there are titular members.

42.

The members shall be nominated by the Crown.

The organizations concerned shall be requested, by notice published in the *Moniteur Belge,* to state whether they wish to be represented and, if so, to furnish evidence of their own representative nature. The Minister shall designate the organziations which are to be represented and fix the number of seats to be granted to each. His decision shall be notified to all the organizations which have asked to be represented.

The organizations designated shall be required to submit within a time limit of two months two candidates for each seat which is allotted to them.

43.

The term of office of members shall be four years. It may be renewed. Members shall remain in office until their successors are appointed. The term of office of a member shall be terminated:

(1) when the normal duration of the term of office has expired;

(2) if he resigns;

(3) where the organizations which submitted the member's candidacy asks for his replacement;

(4) where the member concerned ceases to belong to the organization which submitted his candidacy;

(5) if he dies;

(6) when he reaches his seventieth birthday.

Every member who ceases to hold office before his normal term of office has expired shall be replaced within the following three months. In such case the new member shall hold office until the expiration of the term of office of the member he replaces.

44.

The secretaries shall be nominated by the Minister.

45.

The members of a joint committee or joint subcommittee may be assisted by technical advisers, the number of whom shall be fixed by the standing orders. The Minister may, on his own initiative or at the request of the committee, designate one or more civil service officers as advisers.

46.

The Crown shall prescribe the modes of granting and the amount of the emoluments of the chairmen, vice-chairmen, members and secretaries of the joint committees and subcommittees.

Division 3. Proceedings

47.

Business shall be validly conducted at sittings of the joint committees and subcommittees only if at least one-half of the titular or substitute members representing the employers and one-half of the titular or substitute members representing the workers are present. Only the members referred to in section 39, clause (2), shall be entitled to vote. All decisions shall be taken by a unanimous vote of the members present, unless there is specific statutory provision to the contrary.

48.

Substitute members shall be entitled to sit only for the purpose of replacing titular members who are unable to be present.

49.

The Crown shall determine the working of the joint committees and subcommittees. The Minister shall have supervisory authority over the activity of the joint committees and subcommittees.

50.

Each joint committee and subcommittee shall draw up its own standing orders.

CHAPTER IV. SOURCES OF OBLIGATIONS ARISING OUT OF THE EMPLOYMENT RELATION BETWEEN EMPLOYERS AND WORKERS

51.

The sources of the obligations arising out of the employment relation between employers and workers shall be as follows, in descending order of precedence:

(1) the law in its peremptory provisions;

(2) collective industrial agreements declared to be generally binding, in the following order:

a) agreements concluded in the National Labour Council;

b) agreements concluded in a joint committee;

c) agreements concluded in a joint subcommittee;

(3) collective industrial agreements which have not been declared to be generally binding, where the employer is a signatory thereto or is affiliated to an organization signatory to such agreement, in the following order:

a) agreements concluded in the National Labour Council;

b) agreements concluded in a joint committee;

c) agreements concluded in a joint subcommittee;

d) agreements concluded outside a joint body;

(4) an individual agreement in writing;

(5) a collective industrial agreement concluded in a joint body but not declared generally binding, where the employer, although not a signatory thereto, or not affiliated to an organization signatory thereto, is within the jurisdiction of the joint body in which the agreement was concluded;

(6) work rules;

(7) the supplementary provisions of the law;

(8) a verbal individual agreement;

(9) custom.

CHAPTER V. INSPECTION AND PENAL PROVISIONS

Division 1. Inspection

52.

Without prejudice to the duties of the officers of the law enforcement officers attached to the courts, the State officials and State employees designated by the Crown shall supervise the administration of this Act, the administrative orders thereunder, and the agreements declared to be generally binding.

53.

The State officials and State employees referred to in section 52 may, in the performance of their duties:

(1) enter freely at any time of the day or night without prior warning into any establishment, part of an establishment

premises or other work places where persons covered by the provisions of this Act and the administrative orders thereunder are employed: provided that they may enter on premises used as dwelling places only with the prior authorization of the justice of peace;

(2) undertake any investigations, examinations or inquiries and collect any information they may deem necessary in order to satisfy themselves that the laws and regulations are being duly observed and, in particular:

a) question, separately or together, the employer, his representatives or agents and the workers and members of the shop unions in the undertaking, on all matters, a knowledge of which is necessary to carry out the inspection;

b) have produced for them, without transfer from one place to another, all books, registers, and documents which are required to be kept by this Act and the administrative orders thereunder, and to have copies or extracts made thereof;

c) inspect and make copies of all books, registers, and documents which they deem necessary to carrying out their duties;

d) order the posting up of documents required to be posted up by this Act and the administrative orders thereunder.

54.

The state officials and state employees referred to in section 52 shall have the power to issue warnings, to set a fixed time limit for the offender to comply with the provisions of the law, and to draw up written reports for prosecution which shall be accepted as prima facie evidence. A copy of the report shall be transmitted to the offender within the seven days following the date on which the offence is discovered; failure to transmit the report within the said time limit shall render the proceedings null and void.

55.

The state officials and state employees referred to in section 52 may call upon the local police and gendarmerie to assist them in the discharge of their duties.

Division 2. Penalties

56.

Without prejudice to the provisions of sections 269 to 274 of the Penal Code, the following persons shall be liable to a term of imprisonment of eight days to one month and a fine of 26 to 500 francs, or both:

(1) an employer or his representative or agent found guilty of violating an agreement declared to be generally binding;

(2) any person obstructing inspections under this Act.

57.

In the case of offences under section 51, clause (1), the fine imposed shall be multiplied by the number of workers employed in a manner contrary to the terms of the agreement: provided that the total amount of such fines shall not exceed 50,000 francs.

58.

In the case of a repetition of the same offense in the twelve months following a conviction the penalty shall be twice the maximum amount.

59.

The employer shall be liable in civil law to reimburse to his representatives or agents the amount of any fine which may be imposed on the latter.

60.

The entire provisions of Book I of the Penal Code, except Chapter V but including Chapter VII and section 85, shall apply to the offences referred to in this Act.

61.

The right to prosecute an offense under this Act shall lapse by prescription one year after the date of the fact on which the prosecution is based.

CHAPTER VI. FINAL OR TRANSITIONAL PROVISIONS

62.

Section 3 of the Act of 10 March 1900 on workmen's

contracts of service, as amended by the Act of 4 March 1954[4] and section 5, first and second paragraphs, of the Consolidated Acts respecting contracts of salaried employment, consolidated by Royal Order of 20 July 1955[5] shall be replaced by the following: "Without prejudice to the obligations arising out of the employment relation between employers and workers given in descending order of precedence in section 51 of the Act respecting collective industrial agreements and joint committees, the object and nature of the engagement as well as the remuneration and other conditions of work shall be determined by the agreement and by custom."

63.

The following shall be added to section 2 of the Act of 23 December 1946 to create a Council of State: "The Minister responsible for labor affairs may request the section dealing with legislation to give its opinion, within a time limit of not less than fifteen days, respecting any draft Royal Order to declare a collective industrial agreement to be generally binding."

64.

The following section 5 *bis* shall be inserted in the Act of 29 May 1952 to establish a National Labor Council: "5 *bis*. There shall be a quorum at sittings of the National Labor Council held in order to conclude a collective industrial agreement only if at least one half of the titular or substitute members representing the employers and at least one half of the titular or substitute members representing the workers are present. Only the employers' and workers' representatives shall be entitled to vote."

65.

The following shall be added to section 10 of the Act of 8 April 1965 to institute work rules:[6] "Provided that the provisions of work rules which provide for the settlement of individual disputes by arbitrators shall be null and void."

---

4. *Legislative Series*, 1954—Bel. 3 (giving the full text of the 1900 Act, together with the passages amended in 1954).
5. Ibid., 1965—Bel. 3.
6. *Legislative Series*, 1965—Bel. 1.

66.

Without prejudice to the provisions of section 9 of the Act of 23 December 1946 to create a Council of State, the labor disputes boards called probiviral courts shall hear all disputes arising out of the administration of this Act.

The competent chamber of trade disputes board (probiviral court) shall be determined by the category of the persons to whom the agreement applies.

If the agreement applies both to wage-earning and salaried employees or to persons who are neither wage-earning nor salaried employees within the meaning of the Act of 9 July 1926 respecting probiviral courts[7] the dispute shall be brought before the special conciliation office referred to in section 50, paragraph eight, and before the special chamber referred to in sections 42, 65, 65 *bis* or 122 of the said Act.

67.

The following shall be substituted for clause (3) of section 578 of the Act to promulgate a Code of Justice:[8] "(3) individual disputes respecting the application of collective industrial agreement";

68.

The following shall stand repealed:

(1) the Legislative Order of 14 April 1945 respecting the binding force of the decisions of the National Joint Mines Committee;

(2) the Legislative Order of 9 June 1945 to issue rules for joint committees[9] as amended by the Acts of 20 July 1961 and 28 July 1962;

(3) sections 1 to 23, 27, 28, 30, 34, 35 and 36 of the Act to lay down the rules of the National Home Work Committee (consolidated text promulgated on 5 April 1952);[10]

(4) section 6 of the Act of 23 June 1960 authorizing Sabena to amend its company rules;

(5) section 37 of the Act of 15 July 1964 respecting hours

7. *Legislative Series,* 1926—Bel. 10; 1960—Bel. 7.
8. *Moniteur Belge,* 31 October 1967, Supplement.
9. *Legislative Series,* 1945—Bel. 5.
10. Ibid., 1952—Bel. 2.

of work in the public and private sectors of the national economy.[11]

69.

The administrative orders under the Legislative Order to issue rules for joint committees[8] shall remain in force until their repeal or until their validity expries.

70.

The Royal Orders declaring agreements concluded before the commencement of this Act generally binding shall remain in force, without prejudice to the provisions of section 34, until their repeal or until their validity expires. The validity of agreements of fixed duration containing a renewal clause shall be deemed to expire on the date stipulated in the agreement following the date of commencement of this Act.

71.

Agreements concluded before the commencement of this Act but not rendered generally binding shall remain governed by the laws and regulations which were in force on the date on which they were concluded.

Provided that if any such agreement is amended after the commencement of this Act the provisions of this Act shall apply to it as from the date of such amendment.

Agreements of fixed duration containing a renewal clause shall be subject to the provisions of this Act as from the day following the date provided for in the agreement, which follows the date of commencement of this Act.

72.

The Crown may amend the provisions of existing laws in order to bring them into conformity with the provisions of this Act.

73.

This Act shall come into operation on the date prescribd by the Crown.

11. Ibid., 1964—Bel. 2.

Appendix III

National Collective Agreement of July 29, 1969

Concluding the negotiations for the fifth social programmation in the public sector—negotiations effectuated between a governmental delegation, headed by Mr. G. Eyskens, Prime Minister, and Mr. A. Cools, Vice-Prime Minister, acting for the Government—on the one side—and a trade union delegation, headed by Mr. E. Hamont, President of the Union of Public Services (Socialist Union) and Mr. T. de Walsche, President of the Christian Federation of Trade Unions of Public Services, acting in name of the common front—on the other side—with the common goal to improve the social relations and to increase the productivity, the parties agreed as follows:

I. *Term of agreement*

—January 1, 1970, to December 31, 1971.

II. *Persons and Sectors Covered*

—Employees and persons entitled to public (retirement and survivors) pensions.

—As to the sectors: traditional departments and the decentralized agencies, the special corps (army, "national" guard, magistrates), public and private schools.

—The provinces, municipalities, public assistance and the therewith related agencies.

III. *Measures Agreed Upon*

A. *In 1970*

1.

Restructuring of the salary scales providing for minimum salary of BF82,000 or lower, under the conditions that:

—the minimum salary for an employee of 21 years or over will be raised from BF69,400 to BF75,000.

—the maxima remain unchanged.

—effective January 1.

2.

The amounts and qualifying conditions of the social programmation allowance 1970 remain similar to these of the previous year. The conditions of payment are determined as follows: the first part will be paid during the month of January, the second part during the month of December.

3.

All salaries will be increased by 3 percent, effective June 1; the correlative of (retirement and survivors) pensions will be effective on the same date.

4.

In the departments and public services, where the annual vacation regulation is similar to the one provided by Royal Decree of June 1, 1964:

(a) the average effective weekly working time shall be decreased to 43 hours on July 1. From that date the hourly pay is determined on 1/2136 of the yearly salary

(b) be granted compensational days of leave under conditions to be determined by joint consultation

5.

For the beneficiaries of a survivors pension, the ceiling for calculation of vacation-pay will increase from BF50,000 to BF55,000.

6.

Provisions by sector, by category as well as regional or local measures within limits as agreed upon in joint agreement.

B. *In 1971*

1.

Upon request of the persons concerned and without prejudice to the general conditions, the following services can be included for the determination of the salary.

Effective at the earliest on January 1: the services within the scope of the translation system of the monetary status if personnel from the Ministries, as well as the services resulting in extra pay. According to a fixal salary-system remunerated services are thus to be classified in the immediately lower group than those in which the pay scale of the beneficiary employer is classified.

2.

Vacation-pay will rise from BF7500 to BF10,000.

3.

The amount of the social programmation-allowance 1971 is determined at BF3000, increased with 2.4 percent of the yearly gross salary at 100 percent which served as basis for the payment of the reference-month, the latter to be determined in joint consultation. This allowance will be paid in one single payment during December.

4.

In the departments and public services, where the yearly vacation-regulation is similar to the one provided for by Royal Decree of June 1, 1964:

(a) the average effective weekly working time shall be decreased to 41.30 hours on September 1.

(b) three compensational days of leave shall be granted under modalities to be determined by joint consultation.

5.

Provisions by sector, by category, as well as regional and local measures within limits as agreed upon in joint agreement.

IV. *Specific Provisions*

1.

The government will provide all necessary arrangements for the legal or regulatory implementation and execution of the collective agreement to the extent that the latter involves personnel chargeable to the national budget. As to the decentralized agencies and the subordinated agencies (provincial, local governments) the government will request the competent public authorities to handle these in the same way in view of an integral execution of the agreement for the benefit of the personnel on their budgets.

2.

As to the personnel indicated by the memorandum of the

common front, a joint committee, under presidency of the Minister of Public Employment, will:

—supervise the implementation, application and interpretation of the agreement;

—make all the necessary suggestions to compensate maximally the cost of the measures to reduce the average effective weekly working-time by increasing the productivity and to ensure application of these measures on the dates as determined.

—formulate motivated recommendations as to the proposals concerning the measures to be taken by section, by category, regionally and locally.

3.

The common front will be informed of the measures by sector and by category, which would be considered for the special corps (army, national guard).

4.

A joint working committee, under presidency of the minister of public employment, will be charged with a report:

— concerning the limitations and conditions of a general application of the system of salaries, allowances, and compensations; the proposals of the working-committee may, during the term of the underlying agreement, generate no additional expenses.

—concerning the conditions of compensation and remuneration of the additional presentations. Until the conclusion of the working-committee no changes may be introduced to the rules in force.